TO ERR IS HUMAN, TO ADMIT IT IS NOT

and Other Essays

TO ERR IS HUMAN, TO ADMIT IT IS NOT

and Other Essays

Thoughts on Criminal Justice, Health, Holidays,
Nature, and the Universe

STEVEN N. AUSTAD

RESOURCE *Publications* · Eugene, Oregon

TO ERR IS HUMAN, TO ADMIT IT IS NOT AND OTHER ESSAYS
Thoughts on Criminal Justice, Health, Holidays, Nature, and the Universe

Resource Publications
An Imprint of Wipf and Stock Publishers
199 W. 8th Ave., Suite 3
Eugene, OR 97401

www.wipfandstock.com

PAPERBACK ISBN: 978-1-6667-3823-0
HARDCOVER ISBN: 978-1-6667-9864-7
EBOOK ISBN: 978-1-6667-9865-4

MARCH 15, 2022 11:57 AM

To my daughters Molly and Marika

Contents

Preface

S CIENTISTS can be quirky. I don't mean quirky in the sense of wearing different-color sneakers on each foot (guilty) or in the sense of absent-mindedly forgetting a guinea pig in the hand is not a blackboard eraser (true story). I mean quirky in the sense of noticing things, or asking questions, that most of the world neglects. What mountain summit is farthest from the earth's center, for instance? Is it the familiar "highest" mountain, Mt. Everest, or another that we would never suspect? Is there really such a thing as "sea level," and if so, how is it measured? Why do we celebrate New Year so close to Christmas when it could be any time of year? How smart is an octopus? Why do humans love a well-manicured lawn?

I have spent the last several decades asking such questions in short essays I've written for print and electronic media, mostly the *San Antonio Express News* and AL.com, but a few other venues as well. I've assembled here versions of what seem to me some of the more entertaining, and I hope enduring, of these into this book. I have a particular interest in nature, the parts of nature that are often overlooked. So a number of the essays are about common animals – opossums, ticks, cockroaches, for instance – that seem to me to be underappreciated.

Beyond quirkiness, I am also fascinated by the process of science, how little it is understood by the general public, and how it could transform certain fields that for some reason abjure it. At its most basic, science is nothing more than the accumulation of evidence and its unbiased evaluation, to try to reach the truth. You might notice that this is the same goal to which the criminal justice system aspires. Yet as some of my essays show, credible science is largely absent from court rooms. To a scientist, in fact, the way that evidence is evaluated in criminal trials is, well, criminal. For instance, one simple change, something done in virtually every research laboratory, could at a stroke eliminate crime lab scandals that have compromised justice in city after city and state after state. In the same vein, the practice of medicine also often ignores best practices revealed by science and consequently some estimates suggest that medical errors are our third leading cause of death. Why? Can anything be done about it?

Finally, as any biologist, I am endlessly fascinated by evolution. Whether it is large scale evolutionary events, such as mass extinctions and life's recovery from them, or small events such as how plants and animals change as they are domesticated. Evolution-style thinking not only explains biological life better than any other way of thinking, it is also enriches our appreciation of the natural world.

So I hope readers enjoy these essays as much as I enjoyed writing them. Like a box of chocolates, they are not designed to be consumed at one sitting or in any particular order. Pick and choose, a couple here, a couple there. Fall might be a good time to learn something about turkeys or pumpkins. Spring might bring interest in the origin of the Easter bunny. And around the New Year . . . why do we celebrate it in January when the first American colonists celebrated it in March? I suspect that quirky readers may especially appreciate quirky scientists.

STEVEN AUSTAD, OCTOBER 2021

Acknowledgments

I THANK my wife, Veronika Kiklevich, for reading and critiquing all my essays before I dare release them. I also thank my good friend, and scientific sounding board, Gary Dodson, for his insight and honest feedback when I needed it. Finally, I thank my academic colleagues over the years who have always generously shared their expertise with their curious colleague.

I.

Criminal Justice

To Err Is Human, To Admit It Is Not

I T is human nature to make mistakes. We all make them. It is also human nature to resist admitting that we made mistakes. None of us likes to do that. However the best way to reduce mistakes is to admit they were made, investigate the reasons for them, then try to remedy whatever caused them.

Some fields are particularly good this. The commercial airline industry may be world champion at mistake reduction. You may despise the way they treat their customers, but you have to admit that they are phenomenally successful at avoiding the most serious mistake—crashing airplanes. During World War II when planes were built and pilots were trained in haste, planes fell out of the sky like hail. More planes and pilots were lost to accidents—mistakes, in other words—than to enemy combat. But after the war as commercial air travel blossomed, error reduction, that is safety, became the industry's number one priority. In 1959 fatal crashes of commercial airplanes produced in the United States and Europe occurred about once per one hundred thousand flights. That's a pretty low mistake rate for the spectacularly complex process of building, maintaining, and flying a complicated machine. However, it got much better. By 2016, the fatal accident rate was one hundred times lower, one fatal accident per ten million flights. And incredibly among commercial American domestic flights, there were zero accident fatalities in the United States between 2009 and 2019!

In other fields where complex tasks commonly require the coordinated efforts of teams, mistake reduction could also save lives, but despite serious efforts in that direction there has been considerably less progress.

Take medicine for instance, a study in the 1960's reported that about one in five patients admitted to hospital suffered an injury due to a medical error and that about one in five of those injuries was serious or life threatening. Have things improved since then? We think so, but can't be sure. A 2016 study from Johns Hopkins University estimated that 250 thousand deaths per year were attributable to medical errors in the United States. If true, and other estimates have been even higher, medical errors would be the third leading cause of death in a pre-COVID era—more than deaths from Alzheimer's disease and stroke combined. There were vehement protests from the medical community that this estimate was absurdly high. The medical community could well be right. The important point is that we do not know. Medicine does not have the same culture of admitting, reviewing, and investigating mistakes that aviation has. And of course, if we don't analyze the causes of errors then developing effective means of reducing them will be difficult.

The criminal justice system is error prone too. Now that reliable DNA analysis is available, the Innocence Project, one of numerous groups working to exonerate the falsely-convicted, alone has helped exonerate over 230 people falsely convicted of serious crimes. Many hundreds more have been exonerated for lesser crimes. However, as might be expected serious post-conviction investigations are rare, mistakes are seldom admitted, so we have no idea about the true error rate. We only know that previous law enforcement claims of near infallibility is clearly not true.

How has this culture of error reduction developed so successfully in the airline industry and less successfully in other important realms? A key factor must be that unlike most of us, airlines really have no choice about admitting their mistakes. When an airplane crashes, the news is splashed across the media landscape. As a consequence, all crashes are seriously investigated. In fact, because of the culture of safety that has developed in aviation over the years, even "incidents" or near crashes are investigated too. The main point of these investigations is not to place blame but to figure out what went wrong and to find ways to improve the system so that the mistake isn't repeated. Another factor may well be that those responsible for safety potentially suffer very direct consequences if mistakes are made. Flight crews die in plane crashes too. And so the design of airplanes, maintenance practices, and safety training of flight crews have steadily improved.

In medicine and criminal justice, mistakes are usually not obvious to anyone outside those intimately involved with the events. Also, these fields have what might be called a culture of perfectionism. Medical training, for instance, emphasizes that mistakes are simply unacceptable. If they occur they must reflect on the character or competence of the person who made them. Emphasis is on blame and punishment rather than on improving the system that allowed the mistake to happen. This is a culture that leads to cover-ups and discourages honest post-mistake investigation with the main goal of improving the system.

One especially effective innovation for error reduction in aviation was the invention of the checklist. As pointed out in his 2009 book, *The Checklist Manifesto*, surgeon-writer Atul Gawande noted that people are most likely to err in performing complex tasks when they are either bored by routine or during an emergency when they are under extreme stress. Checklists, if used conscientiously, protect against lapses of memory and attention in both situations. In situations where teamwork is important, checklists which require responses from various team members can also help coordinate the activities of the team and help keep everyone on task.

Modern aviation is awash in checklists. In the cockpit, there are pre-flight checklists, takeoff checklists, before landing checklists, and of course a sheaf of emergency checklists. You might remember the famous "miracle on the Hudson" flight of 2009, in which Captain Chesley Sullenberger and First Officer Jeffrey Skiles successfully ditched their Airbus A320 in the Hudson River without the loss of even one of the 155 people on board after losing both engines soon after takeoff. What were they doing in the cockpit? While Sullenberger flew the plane, Skiles did what his training dictated. He immediately went to the engine failure and "ditch" checklists. Amazingly, he got through the entire "restart engine" checklist, which meant that he tried all available means of restarting the engines, in the three and a half minutes before the plane hit the water.

Checklists can be helpful in medicine as well. In 2001 a critical care specialist at Johns Hopkins, Peter Pronovost, tried a simple checklist in an intensive care unit to standardize the common practice of placing a long-term catheter deep in a blood vessel. Long-term catheterization carries a reasonably high risk of infection. A year after starting the checklist practice, the infection rate in this unit fell from 11 percent to zero.

Later, surgeon Gawande was asked by the World Health Organization to develop a safe surgery checklist for use in hospitals worldwide. With help from a large team of experts, he developed a simple nineteen item checklist which was tested out in eight surgery suites from Toronto to

Tanzania. Major surgical complications in those hospitals fell by one-third, deaths fell by almost half.

Despite such success, checklists have been slow to catch on in hospitals. They are spreading, but slowly. They have not caught on at all in criminal investigations. Why? Mistakes in these fields are seldom visible which means they do not have to be admitted and investigated. There is no way to force it. And when mistakes don't have to be admitted, they seldom will be. It is after all human nature.

Fixing Our Crime Labs

NTHONY Ray Hinton was freed from prison in 2015 after serving twenty-nine years for two Birmingham, Alabama murders he did not commit. The only evidence linking him to the 1985 crimes was a so-called "match" by a state forensic examiner of bullets used in the murders to a pistol found in Mr. Hinton's mother's home. Independent ballistics experts, that is those not working directly for the prosecution, could neither match that gun to those bullets nor even be sure that the bullets were all fired from the same gun.

In the same year that Hinton was freed, there were 148 other exonerations in the United States, including three others in Alabama. All of the Alabama exonerations were for murder convictions.

What these numbers show, although you wouldn't guess it from the popularity of science fiction television shows like the various CSI series, is that American crime labs have been, and still are, in a sorry state. That was the bottom line of a 328 page report done by the National Academy of Sciences, our most prestigious scientific organization, in 2009. Since then, as if to emphasize this point, scandal after scandal has erupted in crime labs across the country.

For instance, in 2017 prosecutors in Massachusetts had to throw out more than twenty thousand drug convictions, because a single crime lab technician admitted that she had been fabricating drug test results for years. A year earlier, a lab technician for the New Jersey State Police admitted to a similar crime which affected almost fifteen thousand cases.

Other crime lab scandals of various sorts have cropped up in Texas, North Carolina, California, Ohio, Colorado, Florida, Illinois, Indiana, Michigan, Minnesota, and on and on.

There are too many reasons for these scandals to cover them all here, but several are worth noting. Sometimes the underlying science is flawed, meaning that test results are never really conclusive, but are open to wildly subjective interpretation. Not surprisingly, subjective interpretation by law enforcement units typically favors the prosecution. This was behind the 2015 scandal at the FBI laboratory about misleading testimony their laboratory staff had given for years about hair and bite mark comparisons. That scandal has led to review of more than a thousand cases.

Sometimes errors are the consequence of simple incompetence. Technicians run the tests incorrectly. Incompetence is the most charitable interpretation of the false ballistics match that sent Anthony Ray Hinton to prison, for instance.

Sometimes errors are the consequence of innocent mistakes. Humans make mistakes. That's what we do. One goal of science is to develop procedures that minimize human mistakes and reduce their impact when they occur.

Other times like the Massachusetts and New Jersey cases above, it is purposeful technician misconduct. In a number of states, including Alabama, crime labs can receive extra money for helping get convictions. If that incentive structure does not exactly encourage laboratory misconduct, it certainly does nothing to discourage it.

If we assume that our criminal justice system values getting the right result, as distinct from getting the desired result, then we should be working to make the system better because laboratory sciences will become even more important in the justice system in the future.

Errors in criminal justice have many effects, all of them bad. False convictions as well as false acquittals allow criminals to walk free. Whoever committed the murders that sent Mr. Hinton to prison was never brought to justice. Errors also destroy people's faith that the criminal justice system is fair.

For those of us in the daily business of science research, it is quite clear that a number of the problems I mentioned could be remedied simply by taking advantage of a standard laboratory practice, one that ironically resembles an old advance in policing. In the lab, we call it using blind controls. In police work it is the difference between a line-up and a show-up.

A show-up is when the police arrest a suspect, show the suspect to a witness and ask if this is the person they saw do the crime. Even in the nineteenth century, it was realized that given only one choice, witnesses often made false identifications. Out of these errors was born the police line-up, or as the British call it, an identity parade. In a line-up as everyone knows, a witness is shown five or six people among which is the suspect and asked to identify which if any is the perpetrator.

Line-ups are certainly an improvement over show-ups, but they are susceptible to their own biases. Recently there has been a pile of research into the best way to perform them. That's a topic for another day. The procedure I'm talking about which would fix a number of the crime lab problems is another type of line-up that avoids these problems.

It is the essence of simplicity. Instead of giving the lab technician a single sample of, say, blood, possible drugs, or bullets used in a crime, the technician is given several samples, let's say three or five samples, only one of which comes from the current suspect or crime scene. The others are blind controls. The technician is not told which is which and is expected to produce a report on all of them.

What does this simple procedural change accomplish? First, it prevents "dry-labbing," producing reports on work that was never done. If the technician does not know which is the real sample, she would not know which report to fabricate. Dry-labbing was the problem in the Massachusetts and New Jersey scandals mentioned at the beginning. Second, if the blind controls are blanks or contain a known amount of the substance of interest or are from a different crime scene, then this procedure should also catch procedural errors and innocent mistakes. So it serves as a quality control measure, allowing laboratories to determine how often such mistakes occur so they can decide if new procedures need to be developed to reduce the error rate.

Certainly most of the people who work in crime labs are doing their best. They are typically overworked, overstressed, and underpaid. They want to get things right. Anything we can do to help them get things right, we should do. But we also need to weed out the few who do not care about getting things right. Application of proven procedures from other scientific fields can help with both of these things.

The 2009 report on the state of forensic science by the National Academy of Sciences led to the formation of the National Commission on Forensic Science, a group of independent scientists tasked with raising the standards of rigor and accuracy in crime labs. Former attorney General Jeff Sessions, apparently not interested in rigor or accuracy, disbanded this Commission in 2017. Politics aside, this was a tremendous mistake. If we are to have confidence in our justice system, it needs more science, not less.

Decision Making on the Fly

A FEW years back as my flight into Minneapolis was about to land in a heavy snow storm, I was jolted out of a trashy novel when the airplane abruptly aborted its landing and at full throttle climbed back to altitude. After several minutes in a very quiet plane, the pilot came on the intercom to say there was a "minor problem" and that he'd be right back to explain. I happened to be sitting in the window seat of an emergency exit row and as we waited . . . and waited . . . for the pilot to get back to us, I could look down through the snow and watch the flashing lights of emergency vehicles as they gathered around the end of our presumed runway.

This is the type of experience that will make you think. What it made me think was at first how does this emergency exit work again? Second, though, I wondered what are they doing in the cockpit? When the pilot finally came back on the intercom, he told us that a warning light designed to signal if the landing gear had failed to properly deploy seemed to have malfunctioned. Either that or the landing gear had not in fact properly deployed. They were trying to figure out which it was. It was night, and with the snow, it was impossible for anyone on the ground to see our landing gear.

Here is what I hoped was going on in the cockpit. I hoped the pilot was in serious discussion with every expert he could find who knew about this particular airplane. I hoped he was in contact with other pilots who had flown the plane recently, mechanics who understood chapter-and-verse about landing gear and the electronics of the warning light system, maybe even the designers of these systems.

Here is what I fervently hoped he wouldn't do—step out of the cockpit, hand the flight and mechanical manuals to the passengers, and ask us to figure it out. That would be crazy, right? Oh, and if any of the passengers had any prior knowledge of airplanes or electronics, would they please not participate in the decision. In other words, I was deathly afraid they might make this important decision by resorting to the jury system.

We inherited the citizen jury system of legal decision making from medieval England. At that time, it probably made sense. A panel of local citizens was no doubt better-suited to determine whether Oliver, the village blacksmith, had indeed stolen that pig or bashed in the head of the innkeeper than the King's magistrate. They would be more likely than a visiting magistrate to know something about Oliver's character, temper, and personal history.

However in the twenty-first century, does legal decision-making by juries still make sense?

We might take a hint from the way science operates. After all, science has spent the past five hundred years developing better and better ways to assemble and interpret evidence to get at the truth—something that our criminal courts are also supposed to do. The last thing scientists would think of doing is turning decision-making over to people with no special knowledge or training in the type of evidence at the heart of the matter. Science has learned to rely on peer review, assessment of evidence by impartial subject matter experts.

The jury system is about as different from that as you can imagine. A group of people, selected at random, with no special knowledge of evidence or the law are asked to choose between two stories, one of which twists and tortures the evidence to reach one conclusion while the other twists and tortures it to reach the opposite conclusion. If this procedure reliably uncovered the truth, science would have adopted it long ago.

The jury system certainly has its good points. It is democratic to the extent that any adult who is literate, a citizen, and meets residency requirements, is eligible to serve. It encourages citizen participation in an important function of government, yet is independent of the government. It also makes for great television drama and keeps jury consultants employed.

However, it's a lousy way to make decisions if you are interested in getting them right. "Justice by amateurs" is what a judge in one of the number of countries that has done away with the jury system called it. Defense lawyers know this. A trial by judge is always preferable if your client is innocent. The crap shoot of a jury trial is what you want if he is guilty.

DNA evidence, developed and validated over the years by standard scientific practice, has revolutionized criminal investigation. It has also highlighted—if more highlighting were necessary—the fallibility of juries. Hundreds of people, falsely convicted by juries, have now been freed because of DNA evidence. These exonerations have become so common they no longer warrant national headlines.

From a modern scientific perspective, the structure of our criminal justice system looks badly flawed, if we assume that its most important function is to discover the truth. The jury system as currently constructed is one issue, but there are others—the use of bought-and-paid-for experts, the inability of those judging the case to question witnesses, procedural weaknesses in forensic laboratories, the use of junk science, maybe even the adversarial system itself. People should have faith in the judgments of the criminal justice system, which I'm afraid they currently don't. I think a scientific perspective has something to offer to help re-establish that faith.

Can the jury system be salvaged, improved substantially by some reasonably simple, do-able changes? I think it can. The next chapter has one suggestion about that.

By the way, the pilot of my plane thankfully did not consult his passengers, but did consult with a variety of experts on the ground and finally decided that the warning light rather than the landing gear had most likely malfunctioned. Our landing was tense but ultimately uneventful. It did keep me thinking more seriously about how we make important decisions though.

The Jury System on Trial

I PREVIOUSLY compared, unfavorably, the workings of our criminal justice system as a method of discovering facts with standard scientific practice, which though not perfect is still the most successful way ever devised to discover facts.

To back up that claim, let me now point out that the University of Michigan's National Registry of Exonerations as of May 2021 lists 2,783 criminal exonerations nation-wide since 1989, mainly due to the development of DNA fingerprinting. Because only a small fraction of criminal cases is ever re-opened to examine new evidence after an initial verdict, this number probably represents a tiny fraction of the actual number of falsely convicted people who have passed through, or remain in, the penal system.

Whatever the real number is, it is certainly too large. And that should concern even the most ardent law-and-order enthusiast, because every false conviction means that a real criminal has gone scot free.

The criminal justice system as we all know depends on police investigators to gather and assemble evidence, attorneys to present the evidence with maximum bias to a jury of citizens—deliberately selected to know as little as possible about that evidence—to try to convince them to reach either one conclusion (guilty) or its opposite (not guilty).

By contrast, science depends on researchers to gather and assemble evidence on a topic and an independent, usually anonymous, panel of experts deliberately selected to know as *much* as possible about that evidence, to evaluate how convincing that evidence is. Notice no one evaluating the evidence typically has a reason to want to bias the outcome.

The parallels between basic goal of these two activities—establishing the facts—are remarkable. But their approach could not be more different.

If the main goal of a criminal trial is to reach the correct conclusion, it is difficult to imagine that the use of citizen jurors to evaluate deliberately biased presentations of evidence is a reasonable avenue to reach that goal.

I became interested in this problem in the early 1990's, a year or so before the O.J. Simpson trial, when the reliability of newly-developed DNA fingerprinting was still controversial. Two of my geneticist colleagues were regularly called to testify on opposite sides in high profile criminal trials. Both were world class innovators in DNA research. Both were reasonable men. How, I wondered, could they so consistently disagree on such a major issue?

Intrigued enough to track down some original trial transcripts, I quickly figured out that my two colleagues actually agreed with one another far more than they disagreed. It was the opposing attorneys' questions that magnified or even mischaracterized their differences, which were in easily-remedied technical details. It wasn't the lawyers' fault. They were doing what they were paid to do. It was the system that was flawed.

Eventually, the DNA issue was settled by scientists getting together and agreeing on standards that were acceptable to everyone. And now it has led to hundreds of exonerations and thousands of appropriate convictions. Why couldn't that kind of impartial assessment have been done in the context of the trial?

Unlike a number of countries such as Singapore or South Africa, we can't just abolish our jury system. It is embedded in our Constitution. Also without doubt, it does have some advantages. It is democratic, but maybe democratic to a fault. It can act as a check on government power and make citizens feel part of an important decision-making process, for instance. But is there some way we could improve its ability to judge evidence?

It might help to consider a specific case.

In June 1986, Ernie Willis and his cousin Billy seemed very fortunate to have escaped with their lives from an early morning house fire in the desert town of Iraan, Texas. Ernie was sleeping in the living room on a couch near the front door and barely managed to escape before the house went up in flames like a Roman candle. Billy was in a bedroom, but saved his life by diving head first through an open window. Tragically, two young women sleeping in bedrooms with no doors to the outside did not make it out alive. Four months later, Ernie was shocked to learn that the district attorney had charged him with capital murder for purposely setting that fire.

There were seemingly several problems with the D.A.'s case. First, motive. Why would he torch a house in which he was a guest, nearly killing his own cousin in the process, in order to murder two women whom he had met for the first time just a few hours earlier? Second, evidence. There was no evidence of any sort to link him to the fire.

Nevertheless, it took the jury less than an hour to convict Ernie, and less than another hour to recommend the death penalty.

Why? Interviews with jurors later revealed that many of them found Ernie scary looking. He also failed to react when photographs of the women's badly damaged bodies were shown in court. The jurors were also skeptical of the fire expert called by Ernie's lawyer because he didn't look straight at the jury while he talked. The prosecutor's expert did look straight at them, even though he had completely botched the fire investigation—forgetting, for instance, to take any photographs of the area where he claimed the fire started and misidentifying all the construction materials from which the house was built.

Does the trial of Ernie Willis suggest anything about improving the system? I can think of two things.

First, how about having unbiased experts present evidence to juries? Judges could solicit unbiased evidentiary experts to pour over the written reports of investigators and present to the jury their impression of the strength of the evidence. This removes the deliberate two-way bias that is at the core of our system as it stands and makes it more like a scientific evaluation.

Second, professionalize juries at least to some degree. A number of countries have "lay judges," people who have received some legal and evidentiary training, that serve as part of the jury. Our law schools and science PhD programs are currently producing more highly trained graduates than can find jobs. So the lay judge system could be a useful jobs program for unemployed scientists and lawyers. Seriously, having even a couple of people on a jury to keep them focused on the evidence and knowledgeable about legal basics could be a considerable help.

These simple suggestions would not make the system infallible, of course. Any system, including science, in which humans participate will make errors. The goal is to construct the system in a way to minimize errors. I think these suggestions might help.

As for Ernie Willis, I don't really think you can call him lucky, but things eventually did work out for him. While he sat on death row, his case came to the attention of a large New York law firm. Some thirty-two lawyers, a new unbiased and knowledgeable fire scientist, and seventeen years later, Ernie walked out of prison fully exonerated.

Tattletale Ancestors

NOT long ago, I sent off a tube of saliva containing enough of my DNA for one of those companies to tell me about my ancestry. I thought I knew my ancestry pretty well and it turns out that I did. The only surprise was that I have more Neanderthal genes—genes, that is, from a species that died out around 35,000 years ago -- than 75 percent of living people. Apparently some of my distant ancestors were not particularly discriminating about their choice of mates.

In 2018 police in California used similar techniques to those the company used to discover my ancestry to apprehend a vicious serial killer some thirty-two years after his last known crime. I've been critical of what passes for science in many crime labs, but the science that caught this murderer was—to use an overused phrase—game-changing.

The first conviction for, as well as the first exoneration from, serious crimes using DNA evidence occurred more than thirty-five years ago. Two teenage girls had been savagely raped and murdered in separate incidents just outside a small English village. Police were certain both were done by the same person who was thought to live in the village. They initially arrested a mentally-deficient seventeen-year-old, who confessed to the second murder but not the first. To confirm that he had committed both crimes police contacted a young geneticist, Alec Jeffreys—now *Sir* Alec Jeffreys—whose research lab was at the nearby University of Leicester. Jeffreys had recently claimed that he could identify individual people from a DNA sample.

When Jeffreys examined DNA from semen samples taken from the victims and compared it with blood from the man in custody, he determined that the murders had in fact been committed by the same person, but it wasn't the man the police had arrested. The first use of DNA evidence in a serious criminal case was exonerating an innocent man.

Impressed with the results, about a month later police decided to try to test the DNA of every man in the village between the ages of sixteen and thirty-three years. More than fifty-five hundred men—every man in the village except one who had an alibi—voluntarily gave their blood and all were cleared of any involvement in the crimes. The investigation seemed at a dead end.

But about a year later, a woman overheard a man in a pub admit to substituting his own blood in the village-wide test for the blood of a man named Colin Pitchfork. The woman went to the police, who arrested both men. Pitchfork quickly confessed, was tried, convicted, and sentenced to thirty years in prison.

Since then, DNA use in many fields has become so commonplace its revolutionary impact is often no longer appreciated. It is used to identify new species, infectious disease strains, determine paternity, identify relationships among species and among individuals within those species, identify remains of terrorism victims and long-dead soldiers. It was used to determine that at least three species of humans, who once lived at the same time, had at least occasionally interbred—thus my long-lost Neanderthal relatives. Former UAB professor, Beatrice Hahn, and her colleagues used its close relative, RNA, to discover that HIV had originated in chimpanzees in west Africa and jumped to humans about a century ago.

In law enforcement until recently its main use was still identifying individuals who had left their DNA at crime scenes. But the case of the Golden State Killer changed all that.

The Golden State Killer, or GSK has he was sometimes known, terrorized several California communities over a twelve year period from 1974-1986. He was a particularly brazen and sadistic serial killer and rapist. In all, he is thought to have killed at least thirteen people and committed more than fifty rapes. It was his identification and capture that has dramatically changed the use of DNA evidence in crime investigations.

Police had stored samples of GSK's semen from crime victims since the mid 1970's, but before Alec Jeffreys invented DNA identification they had no way to link it to an individual. Even after Jeffreys' discovery, they had no plausible suspects. More than thirty years later, this was the coldest of cold cases.

The brilliant new development was that the lead investigator Paul Holes, a retired district attorney, decided to consult a genetic genealogist. These are highly trained people especially skilled in using DNA similarities to find missing relatives such as biological parents of adopted children. It is a complex task requiring much more extensive DNA analysis than police departments use.

Using her special expertise, GSK's DNA extracted from semen, and a website called GEDmatch which links DNA profiles to genealogical data-bases, the genealogist discovered enough shared DNA to identify several third cousins of GSK. Third cousins are people who share a set of great-great-grandparents. Investigators then used traditional police legwork to reconstruct the family trees of those third cousins, back to the common great-great-grandparents then forward again identifying as many of their living descendants as possible. Hundreds of hours were spent searching through genealogy websites, official birth and death records, old newspa-pers, social media, census and driver's license records. The investigators knew the perpetrator's sex, approximate age and physical description, as well as the general area where he had to have lived during the crime spree. Eventually, they narrowed their search to one person, Joseph James DeAngelo, a seventy-two year-old Navy veteran and former policeman. Surreptitiously retrieving samples of his DNA from a car door handle and a discarded tissue, they made the match and arrested Mr. DeAngelo, who eventually confessed and was convicted of multiple counts of murder, rape, and kidnapping. He is currently serving a life sentence without possibility of parole.

The use of distant relatives' DNA to help identify a murderer was something new, something revolutionary, something that has opened a Pandora's box of possibilities for reopening criminal old cases and solving new ones. In fact, within the first six months of GSK's arrest at least fifty-nine other cold case arrests were made using genetic genealogy.

This case does raise some thorny ethical and legal issues about the right to privacy, about probable cause, illegal search and seizure, among other things. However, there is no doubt about its use for solving crimes.

II.

Good Health

Can You Take a Little Good News?

I HATE to be the bearer of good news. It's a dirty job but someone has to do it. So here goes.

We are healthier today than ever before in the history of our species. Despite COVID, despite what you hear about pollution, obesity, and addiction, we are the healthier than ever if you take the long view. We are even much healthier today than we were two decades ago at the beginning of the twenty-first century.

You won't hear about this in the traditional health news, which typically comes in only a few flavors. The most common is "*OMG things are much scarier than we thought.*" Because of (fill in your favorite worry here—COVID, obesity, colon cancer, opioid addiction, texting-while-driving, whatever), we need to take action now to prevent a catastrophe. In rare cases the call-to-action is justified. Life expectancy in the United Stated declined by a little less than two years in 2020 because of COVID and we now stand at over nine hundred thousand deaths from that scourge. However, put that in a bit of historical perspective. The 1918 influenza pandemic reduced American life expectancy by more than ten years.

Disease-focused research advocacy organizations are not going to overwhelm you with good news though. They have a vested interest in promoting anxiety about their particular disease. Nothing like fear to encourage donations.

So I guess it's up to me.

Taking the long view first, life expectancy in most of the world has been rising at a breath-taking rate for at least the last century and a half. In the United States life expectancy has increased by almost three decades since 1900. To save you doing the math, I'll tell you that increase comes to an astonishing rate of six hours life expectancy increase per day for more than a century. For the first half of the twentieth century, this increase was mainly due to improved health in babies and infants as hospital hygiene improved and cleaner food and water became available. Mandatory childhood vaccinations were big players too. That's all pretty good news.

Since then, the increase has been mainly due to better health in everyone, especially older people.

To understand recent health improvements, you need to figure age into the equation. You can't just count up deaths because as the famous satirical headline from *The Onion* pointed out the death rate is still holding steady at 100 percent. We're all going to die (okay, maybe that qualifies as bad news for those of you who hadn't heard), but we are doing so at later and later ages. Most of us would agree that if people are getting sick with cancer or heart disease at age eighty rather than age sixty, we should consider it a health improvement.

So taking age into account by comparing people of the same age, death rates have been falling like hail for almost all major diseases.

Progress is particularly dramatic for heart disease and stroke, both of which have plummeted by more than one-third just in the twenty-plus years since the turn of the twenty-first century. For these diseases, we pretty much know why. Major contributors to these diseases— high blood pressure, cholesterol, and smoking—have been identified, leading to the development of increasing effective treatments as well as life style changes.

Death rates from cancer are also falling and now are 20 percent lower than they were in 2000. That good news is not due to any dramatic "breakthrough," but to gradually improving treatments, better early detection, and also to the decline in smoking. This is the type of steady progress we can expect against most of these chronic diseases of aging. No matter how many times we declare war on cancer, it isn't going away, but treatments for it should continue to improve.

Heart disease and cancer together account for nearly half of all deaths in the United States, so the success I've described so far should be enough by itself to declare that our health is rapidly improving. The good news doesn't stop there though. The death rate from complications of diabetes, again comparing people of the same age, has fallen by 16 percent since 2000. The death rate from flu has plunged by nearly 40 percent too, thanks to better flu vaccines, more people getting those annual vaccinations, as well as improved hospital treatment for those who need it.

The big fat smudge on this otherwise encouraging report card of improving health seems to be Alzheimer's disease. According to the official government statistics, the death rate from Alzheimer's disease, once again adjusting for age, has *increased* by 28 percent in the twenty-first century. Combine that increasing rate with the increasing number of older people and you can understand why there is so much attention (and money) now being thrown at this terrible disease.

But even here, there is some good news. That increasing death rate may be more apparent than real because physicians are more willing now to write "Alzheimer's disease" on death certificates, whereas in the past— before it became a celebrity disease—they may have written "pneumonia" or something else that was the immediate cause of death. In fact, there is some pretty compelling evidence that the death rate from Alzheimer's disease is actually falling slightly.

That evidence comes not from national analysis of death certificates, but from studies of smaller numbers of people whose health has been tracked with great care for decades. In the most convincing study, researchers found that the rate of dementia, again accounting for age differences, is only about half now what it was in 1980. I should note that this was only true of people who had at least a high school education. Education continues to be a miracle drug for good health, including good brain health.

A big puzzle, if this trend is real, is why the decrease? There are currently no effective treatments for Alzheimer's disease. However, risks for dementia include high blood pressure, high cholesterol, and diabetes, the same risks as for heart disease and stroke. So the fall in deaths from these other diseases may be related to decreasing death rates from dementia too.

So here we are—the healthiest people ever to walk the earth with the health future looking even rosier. Don't fret though. There will be plenty of opportunities in the future for something new you can worry about.

Would You Like Some Chirps with That?

A REPORT issued by the World Health Organization recently concluded that eating processed meat like bacon, ham, and hot dogs elevates your risk of colon cancer, and a bit less convincingly linked eating any red meat—this means you, beef—to other cancers as well. Not that the report was a huge surprise. Bacon and hot dogs weren't on many people's short list of health foods even before this new report.

The report got me thinking though about why we like certain foods and find others repulsive. For instance, I like a good beef steak as much as the next person but having unknowingly tried ground horse meat, I suspect I'd like a horse steak just fine too. Other people find the idea of eating horse meat revolting. I've also enjoyed buffalo burgers, kudu stew, and ostrich steaks. On the whole, they were delectable.

Where you draw the line between enticing and inedible foods is pretty arbitrary. In some parts of the world snakes and dogs are a regular part of the national cuisine. A friend of mine's son, who was raised in Korea, once inadvertently cleared out the waiting area of a crowded American restaurant by loudly announcing after his first ever taste of lamb, "Mom, this tastes just like dog."

Most of us would draw the line at insects though which makes Americans a bit unusual. More than two billion people across the world regularly gobble grasshoppers and other insects. One time I watched my wife and daughter gamely trying to choke down a roasted beetle grub the size of your thumb in a Bangkok street market. If you didn't grow up eating insects, they're hard to get used to. By contrast, in Uganda grasshoppers are more highly prized and more expensive than beef.

There are better reasons than your health for eating less beef and more insects though. After all, the detrimental health effects of red meats are small, much smaller than say smoking or drinking alcohol excessively. But it takes a lot of energy to produce a pound of beef. That energy—in the form of the fossil fuels used to produce it—will contribute a lot more to warming the planet than producing something ecologically friendlier like, say, cricket chips.

You might think I'm kidding but a Boston-based company called Six Foods produces such chips, called chirps, which they advertise as containing three times the protein and 40 percent less fat than regular potato chips. The crickets are dried and ground into flour. Other companies are now manufacturing insect-based tacos, cookies, salads, stir fry, and protein bars. There is even cricket sushi for those who prefer their raw meat crunchy on the outside, soft on the inside.

The serious side of insect foods is that they conserve resources, which as the global population continues to grow is increasingly important. A cricket farm uses less than one-tenth the water (California farmers might want to listen up), one-sixth the food, and emits less than 1 percent of the greenhouse gases to produce a pound of crickets than a cattle ranch requires to produce a pound of beef. Cricket farms also use a lot less energy than pig or chicken farms.

Okay, you may never warm up to cricket cookies but insects are likely to make their way into your own private food chain anyway. Some insects are spectacularly effective at using resources that would otherwise go to waste. In 2018 the world produced nearly a thousand tons of animal feed worth about $460 billion. So there is a big market for new, better, and cheaper animal feed. Right now Europe is experimenting with feeding dried housefly maggots to chickens. The great thing about these maggots is that they themselves are raised on chicken manure, completing some sort of demented cannibalistic cycle. It is certainly energy efficient though. The long-term plan is to see how well chickens thrive on these maggots and then expand the program to include feeding them to fish and pigs. In South Africa, the Bill and Melinda Gates Foundation is spending millions to experiment with growing other types of maggots on garbage which can then be fed to fish, chickens, or pigs. We all know that there are certain questions in life that you don't necessarily want answered. I'm now thinking that "I wonder what they fed the chicken on my plate?" may be one of those questions.

The most energy efficient food—either for people, pigs, cows, or chickens—that we could produce has yet to be seriously tried. It lives on resources that would certainly go to waste otherwise. It eats dirt. I'm talking of course about earthworms. They eat virtually anything that you find in dirt from decaying roots and leaves to manure to garbage to soil bacteria and fungi to decomposing flesh of any sort. They are high in protein and nearly 100 percent digestible. I don't know what chickens or pigs might think about eating dried worms, but I am trying to keep an open mind. For all I know worms may taste like chicken.

The health impact of these novel foods will probably not be worked out for a while but the energy efficiency report is already in. Worms and bugs are likely to figure prominently in the world's culinary future, if we are to have a future.

The Chocolate Diet

Y OU will lose weight 10 percent quicker on a low carbohydrate diet if you supplement your diet each day with a single bar of dark chocolate.

At least, that was the conclusion of a study published in 2015 in the *International Archives of Medicine*, an impressively scientific sounding journal title. Sounds good, right? It means that you can add about 250 Calories daily to your diet and yet lose weight even faster.

If adding Calories at the same time you are accelerating weight loss sounds a bit crazy to you, then you are obviously not used to splashing around in the dismal swamp of so-called diet science, a place where you are likely to bump into few actual scientists, but many crooks, cranks, and con men.

It turns out that the study in question was a real scientific study—just a really bad, purposely bad, as it turns out—scientific study. The study was concocted by a science journalist, John Bohannon, and two German film makers, Peter Onneken and Diana Löbl. They wanted to expose how a dreadful piece of science with an eye-catching message could be turned into big headlines by shoddy journalism.

They were certainly successful in this. Bohannon's skill at writing a press release that could be cut-and-pasted into a punchy news item soon led to headlines on *Cosmopolitan*'s German website, the *Times of India*, the German and Indian sites of the *Huffington Post*, and in other mainstream media from Texas to Australia. The pranksters got a second, much smaller, burst of worldwide publicity when they confessed to their sting.

Although Bohannon and his colleagues were primarily interested in exposing how easily lazy, scientifically naïve, reporters could fall for their hoax, they also exposed how easily a piece of purposely terrible science could make its way into the scientific literature.

Superficially, the experiment they published seemed reasonable. They hired participants and a physician (who was in on the hoax) to carry out the study. The participants were divided into three groups—one was asked to eat a low carb diet, another to eat the same diet but also eat a bar of dark chocolate each day, and the third was told to continue eating their normal diet. At the beginning and again at the end of the three-week study, the doctor weighed them, took blood and urine, and gave each person a psychological well-being test. And behold, they got the wonderful weight-loss result that was so widely distributed.

The authors worked very hard to make the study itself, and their write-up of it, as awful as possible. It was small (five men and eleven women, split into three groups). They never verified that the people were actually sticking to their diet. They measured so many different factors on each person that some were virtually certain to differ among the groups by chance. And the paper was written even more inscrutably than most scientific papers. For instance, their graphs were purposely confusing, poorly labeled, and didn't match what was written in the text.

So how did it get published in a so-called scientific journal?

To understand that you need to understand the way traditional scientific publishing has worked for decades—and how it's changed recently.

Science is largely self-policing. Researchers have a vested interest in quality science because it gives their field credibility and respect. Self-policing takes the form of peer review, which simply means that a paper must pass review for scientific quality by other experts in the field, before it is allowed to be published. This process, which often includes multiple revisions of the original paper, generally takes weeks to months.

It isn't a perfect system by any means. It can be compromised by scientific fashion, personal friendships or animosities, or haphazard reviews by busy scientists. Like democracy, it may not be a perfect system, but it is difficult to think of a better one.

Large scale internet publishing has changed—and corrupted—this traditional model of scientific publication. Suddenly instead of academic publishers struggling to sell enough subscriptions to keep their journal alive, there is now the "open access" movement. In theory, this seems a good idea. Once a paper passes peer review, if the authors are willing and able to pay a fee, the article becomes available online to anyone, not just to subscribers to the journal. It seems democratizing.

However, this process has opened a door to unscrupulous publishers, who care nothing about the quality of science they publish, but do care very much about making a buck. And the more articles they accept for publication, the more fees they get, they more money they make. New pay-to-publish journals are sprouting like dandelions in your lawn.

Bohannon understands the new system well. So when he submitted the dark chocolate diet paper simultaneously to twenty different journals (a big ethical no-no among legitimate scientists), he was confident that at least one would skip any serious review and rush it into print. The response was even better (or worse) than he thought. Within twenty-four hours, multiple journals—forgoing any pretense of scientific review—accepted it. For the tidy sum of six hundred Euros, it quickly appeared. The rest is history.

I thought that should be the end of the story. The moral: journalists beware. Trolling press releases for headline science news is no longer enough. If you haven't checked with some independent experts on the quality of the science, you haven't done your job. And readers, don't simply troll the news headlines either. I know it's a radical idea in this Twitter-fied world, but read the article. If you don't see an opinion by an independent expert and some caution about interpreting the results, you should not believe anything in it.

But there is a sequel. I thought it self-evident except to those addled by overindulgence in diet books that any chocolate-based diet was a farce— good for barroom yarns maybe, but not to be taken seriously. In doing the research for this column though, I came across not one, not two, but three non-satirical books on chocolate diets. Truly, the swamp has no bottom.

A Modest Proposal
to Save our Healthcare System

BEFORE I go about solving the financial problems of America's health care system, it's only fair to give a shout-out to Dr. Elisha Perkins, who should probably get the real credit.

Dr. Perkins invented the famous "Perkins Tractors," which he patented after years of research in 1796. Retailing for twenty-five dollars per pair (equivalent to about seven hundred dollars today), his original tractors were a pair of three inch pointed metal rods, which when passed over painful body parts relieved pain and inflammation by drawing off "noxious electrical fluid" whatever that is. Dr. Perkins attributed their effectiveness to the combination of exotic metal alloys he used. Personal testimonies of the Tractors's ability to relieve the pain of arthritis, gout, and headaches poured in.

The Tractors attracted some high profile clients, including President George Washington, and their popularity soon spread to England. However before long, some humorless British doctors started doing their own experiments, finding that wooden rods painted to look like Tractors or iron nails coated with sealing wax were just as effective at relieving pain, so long as the patients thought they were the real thing. Presto! The placebo effect was discovered.

The placebo effect, of course, is the ability of fake therapies, sugar pills or colored water, for instance, to have a medical benefit if the patient thinks they are real medicine. The irony is that at the time of their invention, you were probably better off being treated by quacks using fake medicine than by the actual doctors whose generally accepted remedies such as draining you of blood, that is "bleeding" you, could threaten your health. George Washington, for instance, would have been much better off if he'd just applied Perkins' Tractors for his terminal throat infection. With modern medical knowledge, it's quite clear that it wasn't the infection that killed him. It was his doctors who removed too much of his blood.

So for at least a century, placebos were about the best therapy the medical profession had to offer. With no clue about what actually caused diseases, doctors did best when providing a comforting touch and a sympathetic demeanor, knowing that most of the time people get better on their own. It isn't clear exactly how much of the placebo effect is due to that comforting touch and sympathetic demeanor and how much to the curative powers of hope and expectation. One study a few years back found that people got better pain relief when given a placebo they were told cost two-and-a-half dollars per pill than when given the same pill and told that it cost only ten cents. In the placebo business, you get what you pay for.

Another study left me in awe of the doctors who pulled it off. They asked people with painful arthritic knees, so painful that they were considering surgery, to take part in a placebo-controlled study. The placebo in this case was a fake surgery. What awes me still is the persuasive powers of those doctors. Imagine the conversation with people they wanted to participate in the study. "Now Mr. X, I'd like you to help me out in a new, potentially very important, study. I'm going to anesthetize you, cut some holes in your knee, and then I may or may not do the rest of the actual surgery which up to now everyone believes will help relieve your pain. And, of course, I can't tell you whether or not I did the complete surgery. What do you say?" In fact, they did find enough people willing to participate and it turned out that those getting the pretend surgery got on average just as much pain relief as those getting the real surgery. So in the end it wasn't such a bad deal after all.

You might think that placebos would be most effective in treating conditions with strong emotional components like pain, insomnia, depression, fatigue, and sexual dysfunction and you would be right. Commercial interests understand this and one whole industry—the vitamin and supplement industry—might be said to be built on the placebo effect.

Getting back to solving the financial problems of our health care system. It's generally acknowledged that no matter what the legislative future of health care, its cost will continue to skyrocket as our population ages.

This is could bankrupt the government through Medicare and Medicaid payments. It may also bankrupt those of us with private health insurance with increased premiums and co-pays. And it may bankrupt those without health insurance because, well, one emergency room visit can do that.

So here is my solution. For any condition known to respond to the placebo effect—most conditions, in other words—we replace every third pill, injection, surgery, or other treatment for virtually any malady with a placebo. That reduces the cost by one-third. Then, because placebos are more effective the more expensive they are, we double the amount we charge for them. Now we're talking real savings or real profits, depending on who is paying and who is getting paid. The real cost of medical care plummets, the amount charged for treatments soars. The patients never know the difference.

Actually, the more I think about it, this gets very complicated. I'm not sure who will save money, but I do know is that someone stands to make a fortune with this idea. Worse, I haven't figured out how to get in on the action. Enterprising entrepreneurs thinking about following up on this, you know how to contact me.

Natural Schmatural

I T's natural. All natural. 100 percent natural! What is? Apparently, just about everything. I set myself a recent challenge. Could I walk down any aisle of my local supermarket and not find at least one product announcing its all-naturalhood? Nope. I discovered "all natural" shampoo, make-up, toothpaste, dog food, people food, baby products, instant dinners, skin care products, clothing, soft drinks, and of course just about every so-called health supplement. When I see these marketing ploys, the lights on my nonsense-detector begin blinking furiously.

Why? Because virtually nothing we eat, drink, or wear is actually natural, if by "natural" we mean the way nature made it. We have genetically modified everything. Take that loaf of organic, whole grain bread, for instance. It's a fine, healthy food, but not because nature made it that way. The wheat that went into it is no more like nature made it than my wife's dachshund is like nature made a wolf. We humans genetically modified that wheat thousands of years ago by hybridizing together several species of naturally-occurring grasses, then selectively breeding our new hybrid for bigger seeds, thinner seed coverings, more erect growth, and keeping seeds on the plant as long as possible—as opposed to the previous wheat habit of breaking loose from the stem to be dispersed by the wind as nature intended.

We've similarly genetically modified virtually all our crops and livestock. You probably wouldn't recognize, and certainly wouldn't want to eat, the tiny, twelve kernelled natural ancestor of today's corn, which existed before ancient farmer's began selecting for large sweet corn ears we have today. Our pets, our livestock, our agricultural products, all have been changed extensively by selective breeding—genetic modification, in other words—from their natural state.

One of my favorite misleading phrases of all time is "all natural corn-fed beef." Cows don't normally eat corn, they eat grass, which means that "all natural corn fed beef" describes a non-natural animal (the wild animal, the aurochs, which we genetically modified to become the cow, has been extinct since the 1600's) being fed a non-natural diet that it doesn't naturally eat. You could point out similar things about virtually all of the "natural" products we use.

Nature also gets a lot of unwarranted credit for providing us benefits. It clearly does so, but mostly by accident. As a former field biologist I've been fortunate enough to spending many months living in some of the loveliest parts of nature, from tropical islands and lush savannas to alpine forests. One thing nature teaches you pretty quickly is that species are designed to be beneficial to themselves, not to us. Charles Darwin taught us that. The various and sophisticated ways they do so is the core of nature's wonder. But let's not forget that in addition to its incredible beauty, nature has given us the plague bacillus, Ebola virus, intestinal worms, leeches, ticks, mosquitoes, athlete's foot, and poison ivy. In fact, most of the world's the great poisons, such as cyanide, strychnine, and curare are natural creations to protect plants against their insect predators. Nature, being as inventive as it is, uses these poisons in innovative ways. Some insects can tolerate these natural poisons and even incorporate them into their bodies to protect *them* against *their* insect predators. And some of those predators, frogs, for instance, can incorporate the poison from the plants via the insects into *their* own bodies to protect themselves from *their* predators.

Nature, it seems, is indescribably inventive, but then again so are we. The genius of humanity, you might argue, is in seeing the potential of something that nature has created and figuring out how to modify it for better human use. So, for instance, we have taken one of the world's deadliest poisons, botulinum toxin, and turned it into a cosmetic product, Botox. And some proto-farmer, ten thousand years ago in the Middle East, considered the energy that grass seeds had stored for next year's germination and suspected it might provide energy, that is, food, for him (or her). Then, by selectively breeding that grass, clever farmers over the millennia produced the whole grain wheat in your loaf of bread today.

It's not natural. It's good though—and healthy. Shouldn't that be enough?

Your Snake Oil Score

S AY what you will, Clark Stanley knew how to put on a good show. Decked out in cowboy boots, kerchief, and a battered Stetson, he would plunge his hand into a box of writhing rattlesnakes, pull one out, cut off its head, slice it open and drop the body into a pot of boiling water. Scooping into a glass bowl the liquefied fat that floated to the surface, he would pass through the crowds at the 1893 Chicago World's Fair, letting them see and smell it close up before adding to it his pre-mixed secret ingredients. Of course, audience members were then given the opportunity to purchase as much of *Clark Stanley's Snake Oil Liniment* as they could afford.

Clark had a good story to go along with the show. Some of it may have even been true. Born in Texas, he claimed to have spent more than a decade as a working cowboy before "going native" among the Hopi Indians where a medicine man taught him the secret of making his snake oil medicine. As his amazed friends could vouch, it was a sure cure for your aches and pains, frostbite, sore throat, whatever.

Clark Stanley's wasn't the first or only snake oil on the market. At about the same time, you were welcome to purchase *Tex Bailey's Rattle Snake Oil*, *Rattlesnake Bill's Liniment*, *Great Yaquis Snake-Oil Liniment*, *Tex Allen's Rattlesnake Essential Oil Compound*, or *Mack Mahon's the Rattle Snake Oil King's Liniment for Rheumatism and Catarrh*, among others.

Mr. Stanley was the best snake oil salesman though. Too good in fact. He became so famous that he drew the attention of the United States Government. A decade after passing the Pure Food and Drug Act in 1906, the government analyzed *Clark Stanley's Snake Oil Liniment*, finding it to contain no actual snake products, just mineral oil, beef fat, red pepper, turpentine, and camphor. He was fined twenty dollars and sent on his way.

Because of Clark Stanley and a multitude of others like him, the traveling snake oil salesman, fleecing gullible rubes out of their hard-earned cash, became a stock character in books and movies about the Old West.

Snake oil had no monopoly on the snake oil market though. Other medicinal products went by names like *Dr. Morse's Indian Root Pills* or *Dr. Kilmer's Swamp Root* or *Dr. Bateman's Pectoral Drops*, or my favorite *Dr. Williams' Pink Pills for Pale People*. These cured pretty much everything. Even if you had no health problems they might improve your outlook on life anyway, as many contained opium, cocaine, caffeine, alcohol, or if you were lucky, several of these, all perfectly legal at the time.

Many of our modern soft drinks, among them *Coca Cola*, *Pepsi Cola*, *7-Up*, *Dr Pepper*, and *Hires Root Beer*, were originally marketed like *Dr. Williams' Pink Pills* for their medicinal properties.

We shouldn't feel too superior to those rubes because the purveyors of snake oil have not disappeared. Like the COVID virus, they have spread. True, they no longer come through town hawking pills and potions from the back of covered wagons. Instead, they now invade our living rooms through television, the internet, magazines, and newspapers. Since the Dietary Supplement act of 1994, snake oil salesmen don't have to prove what their products claim, or even what they contain. A recent study analyzed more than forty herbal products from a dozen different companies and found that a little more than one-third of them contained none—that's right, none—of the herbs listed on the label.

Of course as far as I'm concerned, you are welcome to consume whatever you wish, whether you know, or even want to know, what it contains. But as a public service, I feel obligated to provide a guide for helping navigate the world of so-called health products. Calculate the Snake Oil Score (SOS) for your favorite product.

One point is awarded for any product that advertises itself as "natural." Another point if it is "100 percent natural" and an additional two points if the word "traditional" is mentioned. We really should add an extra point if it was discovered by a remote tribe that still hunts with spears, arrows, or blow guns. There is nothing as compelling as health tips from people who lead short, disease-ridden, but "natural" lives.

Let's give two more points if the product features the name of the doctor who discovered it. Science these days is a collective enterprise. One person is virtually never responsible for discovering, developing, and confirming the effectiveness of anything. However, one person can become very rich hawking a bogus product. If there is a photo of the product's discoverer on the package or in the advertisement, it's worth another point plus a bonus point if he—it always seems to be a he—is wearing a lab coat or surgical scrubs or sitting next to a microscope.

I think it should be worth another two points if "*they* don't want you to know about" the product. "*They*," presumably, refers to the pharmaceutical industry which for all its faults at least needs to demonstrate the effectiveness and safety of a drug before they can market it plus a bonus point if a famous university is mentioned. Two more points for each Nobel Prize-winning scientist who endorses it.

Finally, the product gets three points for each celebrity endorsement, because basketball stars and Hollywood actresses are well-known to be incisive interpreters of biomedical science. Besides, that pill or potion is all that's keeping you from jumping like LeBron or looking like Gwyneth.

Add them up. That's your SOS. What does your SOS mean? A score of eight points or less means that this is a particularly inept advertising campaign. They may have put their money into actual research rather than advertising. The product might possibly do what it says. You might want to try it out. For 9-15 points the advertising agency might have done a better job if they had been paid more. The purveyors obviously didn't have sufficient financial backing. It doesn't matter if you take it or not, because they probably couldn't afford the real ingredients anyway. It is probably just rice powder. Finally, for fifteen points or more, you have been seduced by a really slick advertising campaign. The product is very likely worthless, maybe worse. Don't take it on a dare. It might be a good investment opportunity though.

Height, Health, and History

AMERICA's stature in the world is declining. I don't mean stature in the sense of prestige. That's another matter. I mean stature in a literal sense, height. For much of the nineteenth and the first half of the twentieth century, Americans were among the world's tallest people. Now we have slumped to about the fortieth tallest, a little shorter than Greeks, a little taller than Spaniards. While much of the rest of the developed world has continued to grow, Americans have been growth-arrested since about 1950.

I began thinking about height during a trip to The Netherlands, a land of giants. The Dutch are the world's tallest people. The average man there is over six feet tall, the average woman almost five feet, eight inches. It wasn't always that way. Since the nineteenth century, they have gone from being four inches shorter than Americans to three inches taller. What happened?

In the 1970's economists and historians figured out that you could learn a lot by studying people's height. The height of particular individuals might not tell you much, but the average height of groups of people could—particularly about their health and diet.

Nobel Prize winning economist Robert Fogel and his students were among the first researchers to focus on height to indicate access to decent nutrition. In a 1974 book entitled *Time on the Cross*, Fogel and co-author Stanley Engerman used the height of slaves in the pre-Civil War South to argue that however brutally they were treated in other respects, slaves were adequately fed, presumably because this made them more productive field workers. They deduced this from the fact that American-born slaves were about three inches taller than the African populations from which their ancestors had come.

Among poor countries, height accompanies wealth. Countries with the shortest average height are among the poorest—Madagascar, Guatemala, the Philippines. People with money can afford better food, better hygiene, and the better medical care. Poor people in poor countries eat whatever food they can afford, live in squalor, are often sick, and don't even dream of regular medical care.

However, the United States has been consistently one of the wealthiest countries in the world since the end of World War II. So why has our growth not kept up with the rest of the developed world?

People typically have three growth spurts, one as infants, another between about six and eight years of age, and a third around the time of puberty. That first infantile growth spurt will be affected by a mother's health both before and after her baby is born, her ability to provide clean, nutritious food, and how commonly the child is ill. Americans overall don't fare well in the infant growth business, likely because many people lack access to high quality prenatal and postnatal medical care. Evidence of this is that America has among the highest infant mortality rates in the developed world. In fact, we rank about the same, that is around fortieth, in infant mortality rate as we do in height. The Dutch on the other hand claim to have the best pre- and postnatal care anywhere—and it's free to everyone. Their babies grow faster than ours and die at about half the rate that American babies do.

The teenage growth spurt is thought to be largely a function of good nutrition. Americans lag in this growth period too compared to the Dutch and other tall countries. My take on this is what I call potato chip stunting— or as height researcher Richard Steckel puts it "snack foods crowd out fruits and vegetables" in the American teenager's diet. Be that as it may, it is hard to attribute Dutch height to the high quality of their diet as I've noticed that one of the most popular foods there seems to be French fries served with gobs of mayonnaise. Good nutrition is generally linked with national life expectancy too. Those fries with gobs of mayonnaise do have their consequences. The Netherlands currently ranks tenth among European countries in life expectancy. We shouldn't confuse good nutrition with tasty food, by the way. Sweden ranks third in Europe in life expectancy and if you have ever eaten at a traditional Swedish restaurant, all I can say is, "I'm so sorry."

No matter why the Dutch are so tall, it has certain benefits even for the rest of us. One of these is that due to the exceptional height of their customers, KLM the Dutch airline has been forced to add a couple of extra inches of leg room to the average airplane seat. That is a welcome treat on a trip to Europe—even to average-size Americans.

Will Coffee Shorten Your Life?

R EPUTABLE, well-done, scientific studies have linked daily coffee drinking to pancreatic cancer, colon cancer, lung cancer, heart disease, and early death. Considering that caffeine, the main active ingredient in coffee, is a chemical invented by plants to paralyze and kill the insects that eat them, this linkage doesn't seem so farfetched. You can in fact kill yourself with coffee. According to the FDA about a hundred cups per day will do it. Americans don't drink quite that much but they do consume quite a bit. In a typical day, Americans drink enough coffee to fill about forty Olympic size swimming pools. Should we be worried that those of us who just can't face the day without that morning jolt of java are harming our health?

Actually, no. Because there are even more numerous reputable, well-done, scientific studies that find no such health concerns or even a small health benefit from drinking coffee daily. A fair question then, is how can legitimate, well-done scientific studies reach such different conclusions? Are they really legitimate or has science somehow gone off the rails? The answer to these questions can tell you a bit about how science works and also tell you how seriously you should take reported dangers of coffee or the health benefits of green tea or other more exotic natural products.

Science at its most basic is just the systematic and unbiased use of evidence to figure out how the world works. This distinguishes science from politics, marketing, and the legal system where shamelessly biased evidence is pretty much the name of the game. But there is strong evidence and not-so-strong evidence. Strong evidence tends to be the sort of evidence you create—by doing experiments for instance. The other kind, which is the kind of evidence that is used in most human health studies, is much weaker. It relies on observations. That is, researchers ask questions and observe events without intervening.

The way most coffee studies work is that researchers will ask a group of people with a disease such as pancreatic cancer about their coffee drinking habit and some of their other health habits, the ask the same questions of a second group without the disease. They are looking to see if there are more coffee drinkers, or more coffee drunk, in the diseased group. Evidence of this sort can be number crunched in the most rigorous, unbiased, scientifically valid way, but if the evidence itself is unreliable then so will be the conclusions, no matter how rigorously analyzed.

Such studies can be unreliable because not all the relevant questions were asked. For instance, the researchers may have neglected to ask about consumption of other caffeine-containing drinks such as tea or a cola drinks. Or the people may have given them inaccurate answers, either because they forgot or because they lied. Which brings us to the famous Tucson garbage study. In that study, researchers asked a large number of Arizonans about their eating and drinking habits. Then they did a most devious thing, so devious in fact that it would not be allowed today. Still we learned something important from it. The researchers cross-checked what they were told against the empty bottles and food packaging they found picking through the same people's garbage. Would you be surprised to learn that people drank a lot more alcohol and ate a lot fewer fruits and vegetables than they admitted to researchers, even though the researchers had assured them that the survey was anonymous? Remember the Tucson garbage study next time you read about the latest survey of teenage drug use, sexual habits, or any other sensitive topic.

If these sorts of studies can be so unreliable, why do we waste good money and time doing them? The answer is that first they are cheap. You can do such a study these days with little more than a computer. Second, such studies can lead to highly reliable conclusions under two conditions. Repetition is one such condition. If all or virtually all such studies, done with different methods on different groups of people find the same thing, it is probably true. Also, if the effect is very large, so large that whether you asked all the relevant questions or got some inaccurate answers doesn't matter. For instance, what we know about the devastating health effects of cigarette smoking was largely discovered through these sorts of studies.

Getting back to coffee, everything I've said so far pertains to coffee itself. One of the big reasons that early studies found health damage from coffee is that they neglected to ask about smoking. Heavy smokers are often heavy coffee drinkers. Correct for that bias and you get the small, but consistent health benefits. I'm talking about real coffee here—not its various trendy adulterations. For those of you who can't start the day without your triple venti, hazelnut-flavored, soy, no-foam latte, you're on your own.

III.

The Universe—An Update

The (Not-so) Observable Universe

I N case you haven't been paying attention, it has been a pretty exciting last few years for what astronomers call the "observable universe."

It's been a particularly rewarding stretch for Albert Einstein too, even though he died in 1955. For instance, in 2015 astrophysicists made the first observations of gravitational waves, which Einstein, exactly one hundred years before that, predicted should exist. These waves, which I won't even try to explain, were observed when two black holes crashed into one another and merged. Since then, gravitational waves have been detected numerous times. It's easy. All it takes is the ability to measure fluctuations in space that are a tiny fraction of the diameter of the tiniest atom.

Black holes are the original invisibility cloaks. Because light cannot escape from them, they are impossible to see. We can only infer their existence because of their effect on the things surrounding them.

Black holes were predicted by Einstein's equations too.

Black holes are not the only invisible objects in the "observable" universe, not by a longshot. There is also dark matter. Like black holes, dark matter is invisible, but unlike black holes we have no idea where dark matter comes from. We know it is there the same way we know black holes are there—by observing its effects on objects which we *can* see. Physicists think that there is about six times as much of this invisible dark matter in the universe as there is normal, visible matter like stars, planets, comets, asteroids, galaxies, and space debris from our dead satellites.

From now on, I think I'll call it the "so-called observable" universe.

Wait. It gets even stranger.

We have also recently discovered that there were far more galaxies than we previously had thought. Re-assessing photographs taken by telescopes around the world astronomers recently increased the estimated number of observable galaxies from a puny one hundred billion to a more robust two trillion. In case you can't find your calculator, that's a twenty-fold increase. That's like estimating you have a dozen pairs of socks in your drawer, but discovering, oops, that you have two hundred and forty pairs instead. It was quite a surprise.

While it's no surprise that the so-called observable universe is a big place. You might be surprised to learn that it is rapidly getting bigger.

Yes, the universe is expanding, and like dots on the surface of an expanding balloon, stars and galaxies are rushing away from one another in all directions. Not only is the universe expanding, it is expanding faster and faster as time passes. That accelerating expansion rate is due to another invisible presence—the largest invisible presence of all, in fact—dark energy.

No one really has a clue what dark energy is or where it comes from either. Our equations tell us that it permeates all of space, repels objects in the same way that gravity attracts them, and is much more abundant even than dark matter. It is this dark energy that is causing the universe's rapidly accelerating expansion. To make things even more confusing, dark energy did not exist near the universe's beginning. It appeared just a few billion years ago, whereas the universe is about fourteen billion years old.

Dark energy can be found in Einstein's equations too. Like I said he's had a pretty good run recently.

Just so you're clear. We are now pretty sure that everything we can see in the so-called observable universe together accounts for a tiny fraction, less than 5 percent, of the universe's total mass or energy. Yes, mass and energy are interchangeable as Einstein also predicted and as those clever physicists who built the first atomic bomb confirmed.

Here is the strangest part. Dark energy, for all of its mystery, holds the key to how the universe will eventually end. Will it be the Big Rip or the Big Freeze, fire or ice, as it were?

Understanding which of these apocalyptic scenarios is more likely requires understanding a bit about the birth and death of stars. Stars are being born and are dying all the time. They are born when clouds of interstellar molecular gas and dust collapse and congeal into a dense nuclear energy-producing core probably because of some disturbance such as another star whizzing by or exploding. This is how our sun, which is about one-third the age of the universe, was formed. It is a relative youngster, cosmically speaking.

Stars die in a variety of ways as they use up the last of their nuclear fuel. Medium size stars like our sun go through a massive expansion before collapsing again, then slowly cooling. Much larger stars die more spectacularly. They explode, becoming supernovas. After the explosion, the remaining core collapses upon itself to form a black hole. The end result in either case is an extinguished, dead star, except in this case we have a black hole hiding the body.

For a time, most astronomers thought that the universe would end with the Big Freeze. That is, it would continue expanding until all objects and particles in the universe were so far apart that they could no longer affect one another. With no stars whizzing, or exploding, close enough to clouds of molecular gas to collapse them into stars, no new stars would be born. All the stars would gradually wink out over time like the embers of a dying fire. Eventually the universe would be nothing but a cold, dark, very large, and completely invisible space. But more recently, we've discovered that the universe's expansion seems to be accelerating faster than we previously thought. One explanation for that discovery is that the dark energy itself is changing—growing stronger over time—for reasons that, of course, we don't even pretend to understand. This could mean that the Big Rip is on its way.

The Big Rip will occur when surging dark energy eventually tears apart all galaxies, stars, planets, comets—even matter itself. It should be quite a show.

Don't let either of these apocalyptic visions keep you up at night. The Big Rip, if it happens, will happen about 3 billion years from now at the earliest. Most astronomers think it is much farther in the future than that. On the brighter side, so to speak, our expanding sun in its death throes is likely to incinerate the earth long before the Big Rip or the Big Freeze finishes off the entire universe.

If you find all of this cosmology confusing, you should. As the physicist Niels Bohr famously said, "If you aren't confused . . . you haven't properly understood it."

Lost in Space

I SWEAR I am not a space geek. I have never been a "trekkie." I have not seen all the *Star Wars* movies. I never aspired to be an astronaut. I wanted to be superman instead. However, I do clearly remember stepping outside on July 20, 1969 to gaze in wonder at the moon on which Neil Armstrong and Buzz Aldrin were actually walking. I think everyone who was around then did that though.

But after having the privilege of spending some time in the company of several former astronauts and the chief scientist of an ongoing space mission, I may become a space geek after all.

Here are a few of the things I learned.

Maybe the biggest annoyance of living on the International Space Station is keeping track of your tools and other small items, which if not contained or tied down have a habit of floating off to become lost in some of the station's thousands of nooks or crannies. This happened to at least one astronaut's wedding ring, which fortunately was found by accident several flights later.

The suit that astronauts wear on spacewalks weighs some three hundred pounds on earth. Because the government needs a ridiculous acronym for everything, those space suits are called EMUs, which does not refer to the Australian bird but instead stands for Extravehicular Mobility Units.

There is a piece of Velcro on the inside of each EMU helmet so that astronauts can scratch their noses on it. Noses, as we all know, itch whenever you can't easily scratch them, like when you don your helmet for a spacewalk.

Astronauts on long missions exercise at least two hours per day so they can re-enter life on earth with the most of the muscle and cardiovascular fitness they left with. These exercises in microgravity rely heavily on bungee cords. Even so, there are some muscles such as those in your neck that still deteriorate because they are difficult to exercise in space. Holding your head up straight is a chore for a while once back on earth.

Chronic dizziness takes weeks to go away after coming back to earth, because the balance mechanism which coordinates information between your eyes and inner ears is confused by the return to earth's gravity.

For the final couple of minutes before liftoff, astronauts have run out of chores to do. They just sit there and think about what is ahead. During liftoff the g-forces and shaking of the capsule make reading the instrument panel, or even reaching for it, virtually impossible.

Asteroids are not boring. This probably surprised me most. You would have thought that everyone including me already knew that asteroids were not boring since a big one that slammed into the earth sixty-five million years ago killed off all the dinosaurs and three-quarters of all the plants and animals on earth—a pretty interesting (and important) fact. I guess I missed that memo.

Asteroids are the rubble left over from the origin of our solar system, including earth, about 4.6 billion years ago. There are millions of asteroids in a belt between Mars and the giant planet, Jupiter. They didn't coalesce into planets because Jupiter's gravity prevented it. The largest asteroids are more than five hundred miles in diameter. The smallest ones studied to date are the size of a compact car. Because asteroids are small, some have been knocked out of their original orbit and now cross earth's orbit occasionally. These are the potentially dangerous ones, like the one that finished off the dinosaurs. In case you think that we now have this danger under control, how many readers remember the Chelyabinsk meteor that exploded over Russia on February 15th, 2013? That meteor was in fact an asteroid about the size of a large bus. It exploded with a force thirty times that of the Hiroshima atomic bomb just twenty miles above the ground, shattering windows and eardrums over a large area. Of the fifteen hundred people injured in the blast, seventy had flash blindness from the fireball that was briefly thirty times as bright as the sun.

Interestingly, no one knew that asteroid coming. It was hidden by the sun's glare. Maybe "interesting" is not the right word. We do want to learn more about asteroids if only for self-preservation.

I thought the New Horizons space probe that travelled three billion miles on a drive-by mission to Pluto several years ago was pretty cool, but an even cooler mission is underway right now. The goal of OSIRIS-ReX, as it is called, was to scoop up some rocky soil from a small asteroid called Bennu and bring it back to earth. I say "was" on purpose, because that dirt has already been successfully picked up and is on its way back to earth.

Why do we care about Bennu?

Bennu is small, about one-third mile in diameter. Every six years its orbit brings it very close to the earth. In fact there is a high probability that Bennu will collide with the earth by the end of the next century. Since Bennu is about sixty-five thousand times the size of the Chelyabinsk meteor that shattered windows and eardrums in Russia, you might imagine that we would like to know more about it. I certainly would.

Another interesting thing about Bennu is that it is rich in carbon, the chemical basis of all life on earth. When meteorites flame through the earth's atmosphere they are chemically changed in ways that make their pre-earth entry chemical composition difficult to determine. The chemical composition of Bennu, pristinely preserved since the origin of our solar system, could tell us a lot about whether life on earth could have gotten its start, as some propose, from a long ago collision with a wandering asteroid.

So OSIRIS-ReX is now headed back toward earth, where it will jettison the capsule with the asteroid dirt so that it sets down gently in the Utah desert on September 24, 2023. Then the fun of learning something new about the early days of our solar system and possibly about the origin of life on earth will begin.

You have to admit that is pretty cool. I have September 24, 2023 marked on my calendar. You should too.

Round and Round She Goes

WHEN I learned that the rocket launched by North Korea in November of 2017 had reached an altitude more than ten times higher than the orbiting International Space Station, it got me thinking about why some objects go into orbit around the earth and others don't.

The North Korean rocket was pretty much a straight up-and-down shot, a massively larger version of the trajectories of the home-made rockets I used to set off in parking lots as a boy. In North Korea's case after reaching nearly twenty-eight hundred miles in altitude—let me remind you that is greater than the distance between Los Angeles and New York, straight up—the rocket fell back to earth in the Sea of Japan less than six hundred miles from where it was launched. That explains why it didn't go into orbit. On the other hand, reaching that altitude indicates that if launched on a different trajectory, it could have reached anywhere in the United States which explains why it got the attention of the American defense establishment.

To enter earth orbit, an object needs to not only reach a certain altitude, it has to also reach a certain "sideways" velocity relative to the earth like that of an airplane only much faster and higher. For objects like the International Space Station or ISS as it is called, which is in what is called "low earth orbit" at about two hundred fifty miles altitude, the required velocity is around five miles per second or about thirty times the speed of a commercial airliner—zipping right along, in other words. At this speed, it circles the earth sixteen times per day. To picture the space station's relationship to the earth, imagine the earth is the size of a basketball. The space station would be orbiting it, get ready for a shock, only about one-quarter inch above its surface, making a complete orbit every ninety minutes.

The reason that velocity is critical is that earth-orbiting objects, whether in low or higher orbits, have not escaped the pull of earth's gravity as many people think. Orbiting objects are continuously falling due to gravity, but because of their velocity and the curvature of the earth, the earth's surface is dropping away from them as fast as they are falling. The apparent lack of gravity that allows objects inside the space station, including astronauts, to float off in all directions is because everything is falling at the same rate. You would experience the same thing if you were dropped out of an airplane inside a large cargo container. Gravity would seem to disappear inside the container—until it hit the ground.

Of the thousands of man-made objects that are now orbiting the earth, most by far are in low earth orbit like the ISS (and the Hubble Space Telescope). This is because it is relatively cheap to get them there, especially if they are heavy. The lower the orbit, the less fuel and aeronautical sophistication is required to reach it at the required velocity. One disadvantage of low earth orbit is that orbiting objects lose speed more quickly the lower they are, due to the drag of the earth's thin but still remaining atmosphere. As they slow, of course, they lose altitude and will eventually crash back to earth or burn up as they re-enter thicker atmosphere. To prevent that, their velocity needs boosting periodically. The ISS gets such a speed boost about once a month.

Not all objects are in such low orbit though. Global Positioning Satellites, for instance, are in "medium earth orbit," at about twelve and a half thousand miles in altitude, about fifty times—yes, fifty times—higher than the ISS. They would be orbiting fifteen inches above our basketball earth, which I suspect is more like where people imagine most satellites orbit. The higher the orbit, the slower objects need to speed along to maintain it. Our twenty-four Global Positioning Satellites, for instance, travel only half as fast as the space station, and because their orbits are so much larger, make only two trips around the earth each day.

Higher still are satellites like the ones that transmit many of our television and radio broadcasts as well as meteorological information. These communications satellites are a little more than twenty-two thousand miles above earth, almost a hundred times higher than the orbiting ISS, eight times higher than the North Korean rocket reached—about two feet above basketball earth. This, incidentally, is almost one-tenth of the distance to the moon. These are in "geostationary orbit." That is, they stay in a fixed location relative to the earth all the time, so antennas aimed at them don't have to be continuously re-adjusted to track their movement. These travel at a little less than two miles per second and of course circle the earth once every twenty-four hours.

The highest satellites of all (high earth orbit) are relatively rare and typically pay little attention to the earth itself. They are likely monitoring the solar system or outer space or are expired satellites that have been pushed to that altitude to reduce congestion and the danger of collisions in the more popular orbits.

So Flat Earthers take note. If the world were flat, then not only was the moon landing a hoax, so is the existence of the ISS which, I remind you, can be seen regularly streaking across the night sky. So are the global positioning systems in your car and on your phone, not to mention the satellite signals that allow you and your delusional friends to watch the same television program at the same time while thousands of miles apart. If you want to communicate among yourselves reliably, you might consider staying with traditional means of long range communication, maybe clacking coconut shells together or stringing wire between two tin cans and shouting into them. Those will work even on a flat earth.

Returning to the North Korean rocket, its twenty-eight hundred mile altitude doesn't seem so impressive anymore, does it? North Korea after many tries managed to put a couple of satellites into low earth orbit. But today that is child's play. Until they successfully put a communications satellite into geostationary orbit, I intend to remain unimpressed.

Obituary for a Star

I T was a short life, only twenty years, but a life rich in adventure, lush with learning. And now that it's over, it's only fitting that we celebrate the short, eventful life of spacecraft Cassini.

It blasted off in 1997, reaching its intended target, the planet Saturn, seven years later. Most of what we currently know about the rings and moons of Saturn comes from the torrent of data that Cassini sent back to earth for the next thirteen years until it was sent plunging through that planet's atmosphere to a fiery death, beaming back information to the very end.

Saturn is the most distant planet that can be seen with the naked eye, although you need a telescope, almost any small telescope will do, to spot the famous rings. Galileo first reported them in 1610.

Saturn's magnificent rings were first described by the Dutch astronomer Christiaan Huygens in 1655, the same year he discovered its largest moon, Titan. Twenty years after Huygens discoveries, Italian astronomer Giovanni Cassini observed that Saturn had numerous rings separated by gaps. He also discovered four more Saturnian moons.

The Cassini-Huygens mission (its full, official name) provided us with unparalleled close-ups of the rings, which are 99.9 percent composed of chunks of ice, some as small as sand grains, others the size of busses, mixed in with a little planetary dirt. Spacecraft Cassini discovered that far from being as stable and homogeneous as they appear from a distance, the rings were pocked with lumps and clumps, gullies and gaps. Sometimes the chunks collide and coalesce into objects large enough to be called moons or at least moonlets. At other times, these moonlets break apart again. There are even propeller-like waves in the rings caused by these moonlets embedded in them.

Saturn has sixty-two known moons. Cassini-Huygens discovered seven of these. The largest moon is Titan, long suspected of being one of the most likely places in the solar system other than earth to harbor life. The original main goal of Spacecraft Cassini was to deploy a lunar lander (Huygens) on to the surface of Titan. Titan's surface is concealed from space by its thick orange nitrogen and hydrocarbon atmosphere.

In January 2005, Huygens indeed eased through the atmosphere, its instruments tasting the atmosphere's chemistry, feeling its temperature, snapping photos of the surface as fast as possible, and skidded to a stop on a starkly beautiful landscape of mountains and plains, boulders, icy cobblestones and giant methane lakes. Despite a chilly surface temperature of minus three hundred degrees Fahrenheit, researchers still hold out hope for discovering microbial life there one day.

With the success of the Huygens landing, the mission was complete and justly celebrated for its success. It was a star now in the "movie star" sense. Like any star, it deserved an encore. Its encore lasted over twelve more years, during which it focused its attention on another astonishing discovery, the geysers of Enceladus.

Titan is enormous, about 50 percent larger than our moon. Enceladus is much smaller, too small to have its own atmosphere. It would fit snugly within the borders of the state of Wyoming. Pre-Cassini it was assumed to be nothing more than a dead, ice-covered rock orbiting within one of the fainter of Saturn's rings. However, Cassini found that Enceladus' South Pole was much warmer than expected. More than a hundred geysers were seen to be jetting salty water far into space from a underground liquid ocean. Some of this water settled back to the surface as salty snow, explaining why Enceladus is ice covered. The rest is incorporated into the ring within which it orbits. These blasts of liquid water and other molecules critical to life mean that there is warmth beneath its surface and the possibility of life there as well.

As its nuclear fuel ran low, Cassini's directors decided that its final act would be a spectacular one. Rather than take a chance on it crashing into Titan or Enceladus, possibly contaminating them with earthly microbes that had hitchhiked on this twenty year celestial journey, they decided Cassini should make a final, suicidal dive into Saturn's atmosphere, teaching us even more about that atmosphere as it plunged its way through. And that it did, on September 17, 2017. The information from that death plunge are still teaching us more about Saturn today.

RIP, Cassini.

Stephen Hawking

A Brief History

O N June 8, 2018, the ashes of celebrity-physicist Stephen Hawking were interred in Westminster Abbey, the London cathedral where the British bury royalty of all types. His remains were placed beside those of Isaac Newton, not far from those of Charles Darwin. For those of you not familiar with the hierarchy of scientific reputation, the honor of being buried beside Newton and Darwin is akin to being mentioned in the same breath as Michelangelo and Picasso in art, Beethoven and Mozart in classical music, or maybe Elvis and John in popular music.

Celebrity-physicists are rare, rarer than albino tigers or honest politicians. Stephen Hawking was arguably the greatest celebrity-physicist since Einstein. What set him apart is that he excelled both in making fundamental contributions to science and in communicating that science to the lay public.

No one becomes a celebrity-scientist without wanting to very badly. It requires a lot of nonscientific effort and a flair for communication, which Hawking had in spades. His small book about a big topic—the history of the universe (*A Brief History of Time: from the Big Bang to Black Holes*)—sold more than ten million copies, spent nearly three years on the *New York Times*' bestseller list, and has been translated into more than thirty-five languages. It may be the only book on the history of the universe to go directly to film (directed by Errol Morris, produced by Steven Spielberg).

Hawking appeared via a holographic simulation in an episode of *Star Trek: the Next Generation* in 1993. He guest-starred in *Futurama* and on

The Big Bang Theory. His famous synthesizer voice was used in a Pink Floyd song and in a film biography, *The Theory of Everything.* Actor Eddie Redmayne won an Academy Award for portraying him in that film.

Although he would have hated to admit it, at least part of his celebrity was likely due to his unique physical condition. His physical condition, however, made every other accomplishment in his life even more remarkable.

At the age of twenty-one, when he was only a math whiz who had up to then contributed nothing to science, Hawking was diagnosed with ALS or Lou Gehrig's disease and given two years to live. ALS is a particularly horrifying disease. Its sufferers become increasingly paralyzed, finally unable to move any part of their body or speak. Near the end they can become complete shut-ins, alive and alert but utterly incapable of communicating with the outside world.

Hawking, it turned out, had a rare, early onset, slowly progressing form of ALS, but even as he began his scientific career at Cambridge he could only get around on crutches and could barely speak. By the time he did his best scientific work, he was wheelchair bound, unable to write or speak understandably. To compensate, he developed visual methods for working out in his head the logic that he formerly did with written equations.

Initially when he lost his voice, he communicated by raising his eyebrows to choose letters on a spelling card. Later on, he used a specialized computer program and voice synthesizer that he could operate with his hand. He could select phrase, words, or letters by pressing a switch and could do so at a rate of about fifteen words per minute, about one-tenth as fast as most of us speak. He wrote *A Short History of Time* and subsequent books using this system. When he finally lost use of his hand, he learned to control his communication device by twitching a single cheek muscle. The last thirteen years of his life, he communicated laboriously in this fashion—at only about . . . one . . . word . . . per . . . minute.

As a scientist, Hawking was brash, some might say cocky. As a student, he was known to interrupt lectures by even the most senior researchers if he felt that they had made a mistake. He was fond of making scientific wagers, which he congenially seemed to always lose. For instance, he wagered with Peter Higgs that the Higgs boson, sometimes called the God particle, would never be found. It was discovered in 2012 and Higgs received the Nobel Prize for Physics a year later.

He was publically outspoken about many things—his atheism, his belief in many universes besides our own, his support for stem cell research and nuclear disarmament, his worries that advanced extraterrestrial beings might wipe out humanity like we might unthinkingly wipe out an ant colony. Despite his illness, he never lost his sense of humor. To highlight his view that travelling backward through time was impossible, he once threw a lavish party that he only publicized afterwards, so that only backward time travelers would know to show up. No one did.

Hawking contributed to many aspects of theoretical cosmology that are near-and-dear to the hearts of theoretical cosmologists but are utterly incomprehensible to the rest of us. Yes, I'm talking about Yang-Mill instantons, anti-de Sitter space, quantum entanglements, the Hoyle-Narlikar theory of gravitation, and of course Wheeler's no-hair theorem. His major theoretical work was on black holes, those regions of space occupied by matter so dense that gravity prevents anything, even light, from escaping from them. Hawking theorized, and supported his theory with mathematical rigor, that something did escape from black holes, a kind of radiation now called Hawking radiation. Although generally accepted in the field, Hawking radiation has never been detected in practice. If it had prior to his death, he would likely have received the Nobel Prize. On the other hand, detecting Hawking radiation requires the ability to measure temperature differences on the order of a billionth of a degree. Maybe someday . . .

Although the Nobel escaped him, he won virtually every other prestigious prize, including the United States' Presidential Medal of Freedom. In a 2002 BBC poll, he was voted number twenty-five among the Greatest Britons ever. Despite his disease, he lived to age seventy-six, about average for a healthy man of his time. It's hard to think of him as a man of his time though. He was a man for all time.

Cloudy Thoughts on a Sunny Day

WATCHING a particularly spectacular sunset over the lake one evening, it was hard not to think about the future of our planet. No, I wasn't thinking about overpopulation, human-caused climate change, or whether we might be overfishing or polluting the ocean.

I was thinking long-term, about when the sun finally exhausts its nuclear fuel and, in its death throes, expands like a superheated balloon to engulf Mercury and Venus, the planets closest to it, and probably the earth too. Even if earth isn't swallowed up, everything on it will be incinerated.

Of course that's not scheduled to happen for probably another 5 billion—that's billion with nine zeroes and a "b"—years. Or to put it another way, twenty-five thousand times as long as modern humans have existed on earth. So there is no reason to panic. We have plenty of time for that later.

I have been assured, however, by kind-hearted biologists that we humans will not die out in the sun's final fiery inferno. They point out that the typical lifespan of a large mammal species like us is only about three million years. Therefore, we will likely be long gone before this cosmic catastrophe.

The flaw in that logic is that anyone can see that we are not just another large mammal. We have built civilizations, invented science, sent our ships into the heavens, and altered the earth, including its atmosphere, far more extensively than any other mammal species, living or dead. However, even if we last ten—or even one hundred—times as long as the typical large mammal, we still won't be around to worry about the sun's demise.

Isn't that reassuring?

Other biologists—astrobiologists, who think cosmically—have recently come up with a different, equally-heartening, scenario.

We know that the sun has been growing steadily hotter for a very long time. If it continues to brighten at its current, breath-taking rate of 1 percent every hundred million years, then in another billion years the sun will be 10 percent brighter than it is today, which will raise the earth's average temperature from today's fifty-nine degrees Fahrenheit to about 117 degrees. Furnace Earth, you might call it.

Among the many serious consequences of this extreme warming will be extreme weathering of rocks. Increased weathering will remove carbon dioxide from the atmosphere and bury it on the ocean floor. Because plants need a critical amount of carbon dioxide in order to grow, within that billion years, even with the carbon dioxide we are adding to the atmosphere today, its eventual depletion should finish off all terrestrial plant life. Without plants, all plant-eating animals will die, soon followed by the animals that eat the plant-eating animals. That should pretty much take care of all life on land.

There should still be life in the ocean however, because there is much more dissolved carbon dioxide in the ocean than in the air. But in another two billion years, the sun's continuing heating is projected to boil the oceans, evaporating all of earth's water, finishing off any life on or near the earth's surface. Furnace Earth will be a dead rock unless some microbes survive far beneath the earth's surface.

So the cheery news from biologists of all types who have thought about this seriously is that by the time the sun finally flares up in its death throes, we will be long gone. Compared to them, Chicken Little was an optimist.

In truth, there doesn't seem to be a lot of room for long-term optimism—except maybe for this.

In the total scheme of things humans are newcomers to the earth. The earth is about four and a half billion years old now and the death of the sun lies about five billion years in the future. If you imagine the entire ten billion year lifespan of the earth is represented by a clock with the earth's birth at midnight and the sun's fiery death twenty-four hours later, it is now only 10:48 in the morning.

Plants and animals have been around for less than two-and-a-half hours. The dinosaurs went extinct nine minutes ago. Modern humans have only been around for about two seconds.

In those two seconds, we have gone from communicating with grunts and growls to being able to instantaneously communicate to virtually any other person on earth sophisticated messages like "Hey, man, s'up?" We have gone from travelling no faster than our legs could carry us to space flight and from killing wild prey with spears to capturing Pokémon species with Poké balls.

Given that we have come this far in a mere two seconds, surely we can solve this little predicament involving the future of our planet within the next few cosmic hours.

Here is one obvious idea. As the earth becomes too hot to support life, Mars could warm up to a tolerable temperature. We could all emigrate to Mars. The only problem, besides the logistics of transporting billions of people to a place where we haven't yet managed to transport even one person, is that Mars lacks enough oxygen, water, and atmospheric carbon dioxide to maintain human life. We would have to create all these from scratch.

Another idea is that maybe we could relocate to a more distant neighborhood, say to Europa, one of Jupiter's moons. Eight times farther away than Mars and a little smaller than our moon, Europa has plenty of surface water locked up as ice and a very thin atmosphere although it is composed mostly of oxygen. The current temperature is a little chilly—about minus 260 degrees Fahrenheit at the equator, a tad chillier at the poles—but it should become more comfortable as the sun warms up. One problem we would need to deal with is nuclear radiation from Jupiter. At its current level, nuclear radiation on Europa's surface would kill us within a day or two.

Oh well, I never claimed to have a solution. I leave that to the professionals.

So next time you enjoy a particularly spectacular sunset, you might want to spend a few moments musing on these things. If you have any brilliant solutions, let your local astrobiologist know.

IV.

A Little Holiday Cheer

Let's Re-Think New Year

E VERYONE knows that Christmas and New Year's day are too close together. It's time to think about which of those two holidays needs to be moved. I vote for New Year.

It has always puzzled me why we should cram two of our major raucously celebratory holidays so close together, particularly since both of them unlike, say, July 4th, are on arbitrarily-chosen days. Their proximity during the darkest days of what used to be winter not only leads to Zombie week, the week between the holidays when you pretend to be alive at work, it also wastes a major celebration when you have barely recovered from the previous one. If we spread them out a bit, there would be one fewer large gaps between our raucously celebratory holidays.

No one knows on what day, month or, for that matter, year, Jesus was born. We celebrate Christmas on December 25th because the Roman Emperor Constantine decided nearly seventeen hundred years ago that a time near the winter solstice, when the days are just beginning to lengthen once again, was appropriate. Besides, he thought he might also be able to co-opt for Christianity a couple of pre-existing Roman feast days honoring other gods which were celebrated around that date.

Fair enough. Given a seventeen hundred year old tradition, regardless of how arbitrary, I'm inclined to leave Christmas alone.

The New Year is another matter.

The day we celebrate the beginning of a new year depends on the calendar we use. Calendars of various types have been around for thousands of years, ever since people first noticed that the place on the horizon where the sun rose and set changed each day in a regular and repeatable fashion.

From the darkest day of winter (in the northern hemisphere), the location of sunrise and sunset gradually moves north and from the longest day of summer it gradually returns south.

Where the sun rises and sets and the direction it is moving are pretty good predictors of the weather. So keeping track of these things could be a useful guide as to when to plant, and when to harvest, your crops. It could also help you place past events in time and plan for the future.

How to further divide a "year," the time between successive longest or shortest days, has always been a problem though. One logical way to divide it was to use the regular and repeatable phases of the moon. But that interval—twenty-nine and a half days—did not divide evenly into 365¼ days of the solar year, so lunar calendars and solar calendars could never be easily reconciled. That has been giving us headaches ever since.

Our current calendar with its mishmash of thirty, thirty-one, and twenty-eight or twenty-nine day months, approximations of lunar cycles, is based on the ancient Roman calendar. An early version of that calendar divided the year into ten months, each either thirty or thirty-one days long, beginning with March 1st and running through December. Remnants of that calendar are still with us in the names of September, October, November, and December, in which you can recognize the Latin words for seven (septem), eight (octo), nine (novem), and ten (decem).

Those Roman calendar months only added up to 304 days though. There was an unnamed interval of about sixty-one days in mid- to late winter, so later Romans added two months, January and February, to fill this gap. January was named after Janus, the two-faced Roman god of gates, doorways, and transitions, which goes to show that Romans had a god for pretty much everything. Julius Caesar, among his other exploits, fixed the lengths of months to add up to 365 days with a "leap year" every four years. He also fixed the day on which January 1st should occur, timing it to coincide with the annual inauguration of Rome's highest elected officials. See what I mean? Arbitrary.

Like many things the ancient Romans did, that date for the New Year was undone during the European Middle Ages which typically observed the beginning of the year in March, either at the spring equinox (when the day and night are of equal length) or a few days after on the western Christian Feast of the Annunciation, March 25th. American colonists, in fact, observed New Year's Day on March 25th for more than a century after they arrived in the New World before switching to January 1st after our current calendar was re-jiggered one last time in 1752, when we adopted the so-called Gregorian calendar which we still use today. So compared to Christmas, the date of the New Year is a whippersnapper.

Meaning that there is no compelling reason to celebrate it when we do. According to our calendar, Ethiopians celebrate the New Year in September, Thais and Cambodians in April. Calendars based on phases of the moon will shift the day around from year to year by our standards. So Chinese New Year can happen anytime between January 20th and February 20th and the Jewish New Year (Rosh Hashanah) comes along as early as September 5th and as late as October 5th.

Given these possibilities, my vote for a new and improved New Year's is a return to tradition—ancient Roman tradition. Let's re-make New Year's Day on March 1st, which in case you forgot is also National Pig Day. This would significantly shrink the current extra-long gap in raucously celebratory holidays between Christmas and July 4th.

On March 1st, the weather is also likely to be better, so outdoor events will be more pleasant. Also, I personally would prefer to break my New Year's resolutions when the days were longer and warmer.

Hare-Raising Tales of Easter

O NCE our clocks have sprung forward, the cherries and redbuds bloom, and I'm greeted by a melodious chorus of bird song each morning when I take out the dogs, it is unofficially spring. Official spring arrives when the earth's orbit places the sun directly above the equator.

That is pretty much the only straightforward and rational thing I can think of about spring. Certainly the cardinals that fling themselves against my bedroom window every morning in early spring aren't rational. My guess is that they think they are defending their territory by attacking that bold intruder which is actually their own reflection in the window. But after a couple of weeks of hitting the same glass many times every day instead of another cardinal, you would think they would get the message. Testosterone dementia, I call it.

Craziest and most confusing of all, of course, is the Easter bunny thing.

When I was a kid, it was pretty simple. The Easter bunny showed up sometime before dawn on Easter morning and hid colored eggs around the yard. Later that day, you, your siblings, and your cousins pummeled the tar out of one another over which of you saw *that* egg first.

As I got older though, things began to confuse me. First of all, how did the Easter bunny figure out each year when exactly Easter would be each year? You probably need a PhD in astrophysics to calculate "the first Sunday on or after the first full moon after the vernal equinox" correctly. And with no sleigh, no reindeer, no aerial support of any type, how did the Easter bunny manage to visit all those houses carrying all those eggs in one night? And with no elves to help, who colored the eggs?

Childhood is full of these important questions.

That brings up another confusing thing. What species is the Easter bunny? Germans, who discovered the Easter bunny in medieval times, and who therefore ought to know, claim that the Easter bunny is not a rabbit at all, but a hare.

How do you tell the difference? Hares have relatively long legs and long ears like our jackrabbits or Bugs Bunny. Rabbits have shorter legs and ears like the cottontails that you find pretty much all over the United States.

Even though European *rabbits* are not directly related to the Easter bunny, they have their own tale of spring to tell.

In the sixth century, a group of meat-loving monks in southern France, frustrated at having no ready supply of fish to replace meat at mealtime during Lent, convinced the Pope to declare fetal rabbits—those still in the water-filled birth sac—honorary fish. These tasty morsels could be eaten during Lent without guilt. To make sure that they had a reliable supply of these "fish" for Lent each year, the adult rabbits were kept inside the monastery year-round to breed. From these original captives, come all our domestic rabbits today. Your pet rabbit is their descendent. Peter, Flopsy, Mopsy, and Cottontail should be thankful.

See what I mean? Confusing.

Except for the actual Easter bunny herself, European hares are noted mostly for the mating frenzy they have each March, which is marked by spectacular fights and chases. Female hares in spring are only fertile for a few hours on a single day, which is what the mating frenzy is all about. Testosterone dementia, again, in other words. This, incidentally, is the original March madness, having predated the invention of basketball by a few millennia.

Much of the lore of the Easter bunny comes from confused natural history. Because the fighting and chasing are so noticeable during March madness whereas mating is not, the ancient Romans thought that hares could reproduce without mating at all and therefore they became associated with the biblical Virgin Mary.

Some animals *can* reproduce without mating but the Easter bunny is not one of them. The whiptail lizard, for instance, is a species entirely composed of females. No March madness for them.

Bunnies do have a reputation for extreme fertility though. In the spring in particular, they breed like, well, bunnies. This is no doubt the big reason they have become associated with spring, the time of year when the earth's fertility becomes most apparent.

While they may be more fertile than a cow or pig, bunnies aren't close to the most fertile mammal species. Even urban sewer rats reproduce faster than bunnies. Easter rat doesn't sound all that appealing though, you have to admit.

This brings up the most confusing thing about the Easter bunny -- those Easter eggs. Where do the eggs come from? Certainly they aren't rabbit—I mean, hare—eggs. By third grade I knew that mammals did not lay eggs.

Actually, I didn't know everything in third grade. I just thought I did. A few mammals, for instance duck-billed platypuses do lay eggs, but they are the size of a marble, not colored, and never chocolate. Bunnies do not lay eggs though.

My hypothesis for Easter eggs—cover your children's eyes—is that the Easter bunny steals them from unsuspecting chickens. Your children may be receiving stolen property.

I don't make this accusation lightly. I realize that the Easter bunny is well-liked. She has that open, honest face and is trusted by the community. But something is fishy. Millions of eggs appear in millions of gardens overnight. Every once in a while, someone forgets to hard boil one and what pops out? A chick, that's what.

So forget about your coyotes, raccoons, and opossums. The real spring time egg thief is the Easter bunny.

An Unexpected Mother's Day Gift

MOTHER's Day represents the annual apex of high fructose sentimentality. But sentimentality aside, new scientific discoveries reveal how complex our relationship with our mothers actually can be. I'm not talking about psychological or emotional relationships, although those can be complex enough. I'm talking about our biological relationship, especially those cells from your mother's body that lurk inside your heart, brain, liver, and lungs and your cells that live inside of her.

Let me explain.

Your body is made up of about forty trillion cells, each of which is uniquely you. You, of course, being a fifty-fifty random assortment of your mother's and father's genes. But a small percentage—much, much less than 1 percent—of the human cells living in your body are not you at all.

It happens before birth. Every one of us enters this world after living on life support for about nine months in that warm, dark aquarium we call our mother's womb. As part of that life support system, a mother's blood circulation and that of her developing child become intimately entwined so that mom can pass nourishment, food and oxygen, to the baby and the baby can dispose of metabolic waste by passing it to mom.

We used to think that those circulation systems were completely isolated from one other, but researchers have recently learned that some cells from mother's circulation can spill across into the baby and some of the baby's cells can spill into her. A small number of these exchanged cells lodge in the tissues of one another and can live on for decades, interlopers from another person, another generation.

When I say that these cells can live on a long time, I mean a *very* long time. Recently, male cells were found in the brain of a ninety-four year old woman.

How do we know this?

It was originally discovered when researchers by chance noticed a few cells containing Y chromosomes, something that only males have, in blood samples taken from women. Later on, a tiny number of male cells were spotted lurking not only in the blood but also in the brain, liver, lungs, heart, spleen, and just about every other organ in the bodies of deceased women during autopsy. Where could these cells have come from? The most obvious answer was from their sons during pregnancy.

To confirm that this sort of mother-fetus cell transfer was feasible, researchers genetically engineered fetal mice so that their cells gave off a fluorescent green glow, making them easy to spot. After litters of green pups had been delivered, their mothers' bodies were examined for the presence of glowing green cells. Sure enough, fetal cells were found in exactly the same tissues where male cells had previously been reported in women. The opposite experiment also showed that the mothers' cells could also be found in the tissues of her pups. Viola!

Eerily, some male cells have turned up in women who had no sons. Again, the most plausible source was from male fetuses that were spontaneously aborted—miscarried, in other words—so early in pregnancy that the women likely never even knew they were pregnant. Somewhere between about one-third and one-half of all pregnancies are spontaneously aborted, so it wasn't completely surprising. Women can carry with them, potentially for life, cells from the bodies of their babies who were never born, or even suspected to exist. Ghosts.

What are these alien invaders up to? Do your mother's cells help or hurt your heart or brain? Is your mother still making decisions for you? If so, is she working for you or against you? Or could these cells just be accidental stowaways with no role at all?

The short answer is that we are not sure yet. We do have some hints though.

It is unlikely that your mother's cells cause you anything but trouble. Sorry, mom. After all, they are alien cells. Women have a particularly complex mixture of cells, some from their mother and some from each of their live-born and miscarried children—a regular family dinner table of cells. Like many family dinners, things may not always go well. The cells of your immune system are always patrolling for alien invaders to attack. Encountering alien cells—even though they may be from your relatives—so often might make your immune system a bit trigger happy, liable to attack on the slightest provocation. Your cells, innocent bystanders in other words, could get hurt. This familial mixture of cells could help explain why women are particularly prone to autoimmune diseases, diseases like juvenile diabetes, lupus, or multiple sclerosis in which your immune system mistakenly attacks your own cells.

On the other hand, fetal cells may be quite useful to mommy dearest. Fetal cells have remarkable abilities to regenerate and repair tissue damage. For instance, wounds to fetal skin heal quickly without a trace of a scar during the first two trimesters of pregnancy. In one study, experimenters damaged the hearts of pregnant mice and noticed that cells from their fetuses homed in on the site of injury and repaired it. From this and other mouse studies, we know that these alien fetal cells can be transformed into actual heart and brain cells. No one has shown that in people yet, but there is little reason to doubt that the same happens in us.

So if you forgot to get your mom a present this past Mother's Day, you might try make up for it by reminding her how her healthy heart, her fondness for crossword puzzles, and her great sense of humor may in fact be due to that present of healthy heart and brain cells that you gave her before you were even born. Before you do this, however, I would be very, very sure that your mother really does have a great sense of humor.

Our Pumpkin Problem

A UTUMN is the season of the jack-o'-lantern, pumpkin pie, and the pumpkin spiced latté. Pumpkins, unlike turkey and cranberries, were likely on the menu of the first American Thanksgiving in the autumn of 1621. So given its place in our history and culture you might think that it should be pretty evident what a pumpkin is. You would be wrong.

The mental picture of a pumpkin that most people, including me, conjure up is the basketball-size orange fruit that we carve into scary faces around Halloween. Yes, I said "fruit." Pumpkins contain seeds, a defining feature of fruits. Tomatoes, for instance, are fruits too.

Fleshy fruits like pumpkins are meant to be eaten by nonhuman animals. Fruits are nature's way of providing animals a nutritious reward for swallowing their seeds and dispersing them far and wide. At some distance from their birth place, they emerge from the animals' other end, fall into the soil packed in fertilizer, and with luck eventually grow into a new plant.

For this plant strategy to work, the seeds need to be fully developed when the fruit is eaten. Plants manage this by making fruits taste awful prior to the seeds being ready as anyone who has bitten into an unripe fruit can attest. Also, plants need to discourage animals from chewing up—that is, killing—the seeds before swallowing them. Plants do this by packing seeds with foul tasting, potentially toxic chemicals which can be largely avoided if the seeds are swallowed whole. So for you campers eager to try subsisting on wild fruit, first be very careful—some of those fruits will poison you—and second when in doubt spit out or swallow the seeds, don't chew them.

By now you might be wondering what sort of animal would (or could) eat something the size of a pumpkin without chewing up their dime-size seeds, which brings us to mastodons.

Mastodons you may recall were North America's elephants. They looked a lot like a modern Asian elephant except they were thickly furred. They appeared around five million years ago and disappeared about ten thousand years ago, not long after people first arrived on this continent. Mastodons loved to dine on pumpkins.

Well, not pumpkins exactly. They dined on pumpkins' wild ancestor, the avocado-size wild squash. We know this because biologists who study the ecology of ancient times love to pick through ancient dung whenever and wherever they can find it. Mastodons left around a lot of dung, which has been picked through extensively and intact wild squash seeds have been found there in abundance.

Wild squash like any self-respecting plant protects its seeds with bitter tasting, toxic chemicals, but recent research which examined mastodons' DNA suggests that mastodons lacked the taste buds to sense those bitter-tasting chemicals. Also, the mammoths' enormous size would have protected them against eating enough wild squash to make them really sick.

So pumpkins are a domesticated version of the wild squash, from which ancient farmers bred out the toxic, bitter-tasting chemicals. Here the first pumpkin problem though. There are numerous other domesticated versions of the same wild squash species, including summer squash, several types of winter squash, spaghetti squash, acorn squash, and zucchini, all of which have had the toxins—at least those toxins resistant to cooking—bred out of them. A jack-o'-lantern pumpkin is a breed of wild squash in the same way that a Great Dane, Labrador retriever, or pug is a breed of dog.

Because all these squashes are a single species, they can all interbreed. If you pollinate a pumpkin flower with zucchini pollen or vice versa, you will end up with a fruit that is something in between the two. Maybe call it a pump-kini? Worse, if you pollinate any of these domestic squashes with pollen from a wild squash, you will end up with a fruit that is bitter-tasting and toxic like wild squash, which is why we owe mastodons a bit of gratitude for going extinct.

When mastodons roamed the American forests, wild squash were abundant. So abundant that if people had tried to domesticate them into something edible, their pollinators—native American bees, honey bees only arrived with the first European colonists—would have no doubt often dusted them with the pollen from wild squash, keeping them inedible. Squash are one of the oldest domesticated crops, predating the Pilgrims by thousands of years. At that time, people had no inkling about pollination biology, so they would never have figured out why despite their best efforts to selectively breed sweet-tasting squash, it continued to have that foul taste. However, wild squash numbers fell dramatically when mastodons, their chief seed disperser, vanished. Once the wild squash was rare enough, the chances of wild pollen-carrying bees landing on plants that people were selectively breeding for their size and taste became remote. Domestication of all those squash varieties could proceed.

So now you may think you know what a pumpkin is—a large orange domesticated breed of wild squash that we carve into scary faces. Not so fast. That is the jack-o'-lantern pumpkin. The canned "pumpkin" filling that we use to make pies and spiced lattés is a completely different species, one that is South American rather than North American in origin! The pie-filling pumpkin is the same species that includes another breed we call butternut squash. So a zucchini is more closely related to your jack-o'-lantern than is the filling in your pumpkin pie. What's more, those giant "pumpkins" that farmers are always winning prizes for growing are yet a third species, also South American.

So, what is a pumpkin? I'm not longer sure. Maybe you can tell me?

Tribute to the Turkey

ONCE a year—I suggest the day after Thanksgiving—it is only fit and proper that we pause for a moment of silence for those fifty million turkeys that sacrificed their lives so that we could doze through holiday football in a satisfied, gluttonous haze.

If that sounds like a lot of turkeys, it is. That number of turkeys standing as closely packed as possible without jostling one another would occupy about three square miles or fifteen hundred football fields. Over the course of a year, Americans eat more than two hundred million turkeys, which also seems like a lot until you consider that we eat more than eight *billion* chickens per year.

Of course—delicious as they are—we don't eat real turkeys on Thanksgiving. We eat their cousins, which were domesticated by the Aztecs in Mexico more than two thousand years ago. Conquistadores hauled the domesticated turkey back to Europe in the early 1500's, where they spread rapidly because of the popularity of their meat, eggs, and feathers, eventually making their way to England, where they got their English name due to a misidentification. The English thought they were African guineafowl, another plump, tasty ground bird species with colorful head ornaments, African guineafowl in those days were commonly imported from Turkey. And so they were called "Turkey fowl." We now eat a quintessentially American bird domesticated in Mexico and named after a Eurasian country which it never inhabited.

Domesticated turkeys were reimported to the Americas with some of the first English colonists, maybe even the very first colonists, those of Jamestown not the late-comers in Plymouth, Massachusetts. Ironically, it isn't clear that turkeys were actually eaten at that first Thanksgiving. The only contemporary account of that meal by Edward Winslow describes only that they ate "fowl," which could have been ducks, geese, swans, or cranes as easily as turkeys.

Like almost everything else we've domesticated, the turkey that most of us eat is a bizarre creature. We have for centuries now selected it for those large tasty breast muscles, which are so large that they are no longer useful for their primary purpose, which was to fly. Wild turkeys routinely fly short distances. In fact, they roost in trees. But domesticated turkeys are earthbound. We've also selected for large, bulky thigh muscles because of our love of drumsticks. So domestic turkeys run awkwardly at best. One thing that hasn't changed is muscle—that is, meat—color. White muscle is designed for short bursts of energy. Wild turkeys use their breast muscles to flap their wings rapidly for short bursts of flight. Dark muscle is dark because it is packed with energy-storing molecules, which prime that muscle for endurance. Wild turkeys can run for much longer than they can fly. And so turkey breast meat is white, drumstick meat is dark.

In my current home state of Alabama, we are fortunate to have plenty of wild turkeys. These elegant dark-colored birds can be heard gobbling in the forest in the spring. This is the sound of males courting. Male turkeys are in fact properly known as gobblers. During this breeding period males may also develop iridescent red, green, gold, or copper-colored plumage to help attract females. By summer you will see hens followed by their flock of chicks, and in the fall and winter you might see flocks of dozens of turkeys of both sexes foraging for acorns, hickory, and beech nuts on the ground. As is well-known albeit apocryphal, Benjamin Franklin considered the wild turkey so majestic that he favored it over the bald eagle as our national symbol.

The domestic turkey is a different story altogether. In a past life, I spent several weeks each fall making daily visits to a California turkey farm, that just before Thanksgiving held nearly a million birds. These birds were pure white, deafeningly noisy, and spectacularly stupid. The reason I visited the farm each afternoon was to retrieve carcasses of birds that were trampled to death in the turkey stampede that invariably accompanied the appearance of the feed truck. These carcasses served a good purpose though. The big cats, lions and tigers, I was caring for loved them. They would eat everything, bones and feathers included.

It is difficult for me to avoid concluding that these domesticated birds are the reason that the whole species gets so little respect. After all, think of how we take their name in vain. A failed show business production or hopelessly inept person is a turkey. Game hunting too easy to be worth the effort is a turkey shoot. Nonsensical speech like that of politicians is called gobbledygook.

But autumn is a season for charity and good will. Let's thank those fifty million turkeys. They might have lacked dignity in life, but they certainly enrich our holiday on the platter.

Tough Times for Santa

LIKE many of you, I'm a little concerned about Santa Claus these days. Although the exact location of his residence is a closely-guarded secret, like his age, we know it is somewhere in the vicinity of the North Pole. As the Arctic ice cap continues to melt with increasing global temperatures, wherever he lives up there, it is possible that his house and workshop could one day crash through the thinning ice and vanish beneath the sea. That would certainly disappoint a lot of well-behaved children.

I'm hoping though that he had sense enough to build his house on land rather than on the ever shifting and drifting sea ice found around the actual North Pole. In fact, I'm pretty sure that's what he did, based on the evidence of his reindeer.

You may recall from Clement Moore's famous 1823 poem, *'Twas the Night Before Christmas*, that Santa drove a miniature sleigh drawn by "eight tiny reindeer." The makes me think that he may hide out between holiday seasons somewhere on Svalbard, an island archipelago about halfway between Norway and the North Pole.

Reindeer—we call them caribou in North America—are the second largest deer species on earth. The only larger species is the moose. That is, the only larger species is the one we North Americans call a moose. The English call them elk. What we call elk, of course, the British call something else—red deer to be exact. We can thank early British colonists, not the most accomplished naturalists, for such terminological confusion about our animals. We should be glad that they didn't confuse mouse with moose.

Getting back to reindeer, an average male, called a bull, weighs as much as four hundred pounds, a typical female or doe weighs about half that. Maybe Santa's "miniature reindeer" were all female. Reindeer are the only species of deer in which both sexes have antlers, so to a casual observer an all-doe team might have looked like a group of miniatures. Besides eight females wouldn't be so likely to squabble over who gets to lead the team. On the other hand, even eight two hundred pound reindeer plus Santa plus his sleigh with all the presents—that's several tons at least—landing on your roof could be problematic, which is why I favor the Svalbard idea.

Reindeer on the Svalbard islands like animals on many islands, and like Santa's elves, are dwarfs. They weigh only about half as much as reindeer on the mainland. So maybe Santa's hideaway is on Svalbard where melting sea ice would not send his house and workshop to the bottom of the ocean. Eight one hundred pound does plus Santa plus his sleigh with all the presents might still seem problematic in the roof-landing department, but compared to teaching reindeer to fly without wings while towing a heavy sleigh, it must be a cinch.

The other problem Santa is no doubt confronting is pressure to install a Global Positioning System, or GPS, in his sleigh. As we all know that a GPS is a satellite-based navigation system designed to destroy any sense of direction you may have previously had. Santa apparently managed to find all the children before there was a GPS, even after his route expanded a few centuries ago from Europe to include North America. In all that time, I've never heard reports of him stopping to ask for directions. As a self-respecting old school male, I know for a fact that he wouldn't stop to ask directions no matter how temporarily confused he might be. For those without any sense of direction, GPS may be a necessary crutch. However, for those of us like Santa who are perfectly capable of finding our own way no matter how long it takes, relying on a GPS is only slightly less emasculating than asking for directions. Let's hope that Santa continues to resist the dreaded GPS-assisted delivery and rely on his own instincts. He owes it to the other males on the planet.

V.

The Nature of Nature

Getting High Nature's Way

OST of us are at least a little familiar with the challenges of climbing Mt. Everest, the world's highest terrestrial peak—the months of training, weeks of acclimatization, temperatures seriously below zero, one-third as much oxygen in each breath as at sea level, snow streaming off the summit like smoke from life-threatening jet stream winds. And yet some hardy climbers with their guides, their Sherpa support team, their oxygen bottles, their high-tech tents and high-tech clothing struggle step by painful step to Everest's summit. Amazing.

A lot more amazing to my mind though are the geese that fly by, or even over, the highest human climbers. These geese, bar-headed geese to be precise, don't struggle to make the simplest movements at this altitude. Without training, without acclimatization, without special clothes or oxygen masks, beating their wings a steady 4-5 times per second hour after hour, they take off from sea level in India, climb nearly thirty thousand feet in altitude, and cross the highest Himalayas less than twenty-four hours later on their way to their Siberian breeding grounds.

Seeing birds every day, it is easy to forget how remarkable they are. The bar-headed goose, of course, is particularly remarkable for its high altitude endurance feats. Other birds perform equally amazing feats. A wading bird called the bar-tailed godwit flies nonstop for nine straight days and nights without re-fueling, that is without stopping to eat or drink, in a seven thousand mile migration from Alaska to New Zealand. That, by the way, is within shouting distance of the world's longest nonstop commercial airline flight.

But even a standard-issue sparrow can perform physical feats that would humble the most highly trained human.

Take the house sparrow, for instance, the most common bird you are likely to see in cities in towns around the world, and compare it to the similar-sized house mouse, the most common rodent you are likely to find in your pantry around the world. Put each one in a chamber that can simulate the atmospheric conditions of different altitudes. At sea level, both are alert and inquisitive. Reducing the oxygen to the equivalent of an altitude of thirteen thousand feet makes the mouse lethargic but has no apparent effect on the sparrow. Incidentally, travelling from sea level to thirteen thousand feet within a few minutes would make you feel poorly as well.

Continue to reduce the chamber's oxygen level and when it reaches the equivalent of twenty thousand feet altitude, the sparrow will still be perky and alert although its heart and breathing rates will have doubled to keep enough oxygen flowing to its brain and other organs. The mouse by this time is comatose. Its heart and breathing rates have both dropped dangerously. If not removed from the chamber, it will die.

The point is that you don't have to climb the Himalayas to see amazing birds. They are around you daily. You just need to learn to appreciate them.

Which brings me to our hummingbird. I say "our hummingbird" because for those of us who live in the United States east of the Mississippi river anywhere from the Gulf coast to southern Canada, there is only one hummingbird species, the ruby-throated hummingbird, so named because of the males' brilliantly iridescent red throat. Our hummingbird is tiny. It weighs just a bit more than a penny, no bigger than a large moth. It consumes a mostly liquid diet, nectar from flowers or your backyard feeder supplemented with the occasional insect.

The name hummingbird itself comes from the low-pitched hum they make in flight. The hum comes from their wing beats of up to seventy times per second in normal flight, which is about the vibration frequency of a low C note on a piano. Their wings are a barely visible blur. Hummingbirds are also unique in that, because they can flip their wings upside down, they can fly forward, backward, or even hover in mid-air.

When you see a bird in which the males are more ornately feathered than females, our hummingbird's ruby throat, for instance, or the peacock's elaborate tail, nature is telling you that the males take no part in parenting. So females are not looking for helpful partners when they mate in these species. They are looking for a provider of good genes for the chicks. Male hummingbirds make their genetic case by showing off. During incredible courtship displays of aerial agility, they dive, dip, and swoop, accelerating their wing beats at times up to two hundred times per second.

This remarkable hummingbird flight requires powerful muscles and massive amounts of energy. The pectoral or flight muscles comprise one-quarter of a hummingbird's total weight. Per gram of muscle, they use energy at more than ten times the rate that elite human athletes use energy during intense exercise. Energy requires fuel, sugar and oxygen in this case. To meet their energy demands, hummingbirds drink up to several times their body weight in nectar each day, loading their blood with so much sugar that they would be dangerously diabetic if they were human. Oxygen is supplied by breathing two hundred fifty times per minute, faster than a dog pants, and passing that air through exceptionally efficient lungs. Oxygen- and sugar-loaded blood is pumped to their muscles, brain, and other tissues by a heart that is five times the size of ours relative to their size. That heart beats at a machinegun-like twenty times per second.

Because of these high energy needs, hummingbirds cannot go long periods without food. As flowers wilt and insects begin to disappear at the end of summer, our hummingbirds must head south. They winter in southern Mexico and Central America where flowers bloom and insects abound year-round.

Now comes perhaps their most remarkable feat. As they prepare for migration, they begin to pack on fuel in the form of fat. Within a couple of weeks, they turn from sleek athletes into butterballs, adding enough fat to double their body weight as they ready for a life-or-death flight. These tiny, moth-size birds now attempt to fly nonstop more than five hundred miles across the Gulf of Mexico. The trip takes about twenty hours if weather conditions are good and if the birds are in good enough condition to make it. If you're keeping track that journey requires more than five million wingbeats in less than a day. The ones that do make it will have lost more than half their body weight in less than a day. Call it the Gulf crash diet. They not only take the weight off, they keep it off—at least for a few months.

Come spring, they will make the return journey. Bulking up again and losing it again in that dramatic ocean crossing. You might think that such an intense lifestyle would burn them out quickly, but some hummingbirds survive long enough to make that Gulf crossing nearly twenty times.

So the next time you see one of our hummingbirds pause a second and give a mental tip of the cap to one of nature's most remarkable creatures.

The Remarkable Opossum

U NLIKE the cliché, familiarity doesn't seem to breed contempt. It breeds indifference. Why else would we take so little interest in one of the most fascinating of America's wildlife, the opossum?

That's opossum with an "o" and that "o" is important. To be technically correct, it's the Virginia, as in the State, opossum and that "Virginia" is important too. The Virginia opossum got this common name from its Algonquian Indian name "apasum," meaning "white beast," and from the state where it was first given an English name in the early 1600's by Captain John Smith of the Jamestown Colony and Pocahontas fame.

The "o" is important because when British explorer James Cook, on his first voyage to Australia a century and a half after Captain Smith named them, encountered other cat-sized animals that nurtured their young in a pouch, his ship's naturalist erroneously assumed they were the same, or at least similar, species and called them opossums too. It turns out that the Australian marsupials are not closely related to our opossums, so to prevent confusion, scientists now call all Australian species possums—no "o"—to distinguish them from our opossums.

The "Virginia" is important for another reason. Although we only have one marsupial species in the United States, more than seventy more species occur throughout Central and South America. So in addition to our Virginia opossum, there are mouse opossums, slender opossums, water opossums, pygmy opossums, and woolly opossums, not to mention fat-, short-, thick-, and bushy-tailed opossums, plus my favorite, four-eyed opossums.

They are all marsupials though, animals that give birth to still developing embryonic pups and rear them for months in a pouch. Virginia opossums are pregnant for only twelve days before giving birth to ten to fifty of these pups, each about the size of a large ant. In order to survive, these deaf, blind, hairless fetuses have to crawl unaided the inch or so from their mother's birth canal into her pouch and find one of her thirteen nipples. As only 5-7 young are typically raised, many pups are lost along the way. For those lucky enough to find and attach to a nipple, their lips soon fuse together and for the next two months they remain continuously fastened to that nipple. If dislodged, they will be unable to re-attach and will die. Life is no picnic for an opossum pup.

By the time they are three to four months old, opossums have left the pouch for good and are on their own. Also by this time, they've acquired all those traits which make them such endearing creatures. They have all fifty of their teeth, most of any American mammal, which they use to eat your garbage, your pet's food if you leave it outdoors, or just about any food that won't eat them first. They have hind feet with opposable thumbs, and they are the only mammal native to the United States with a grasping prehensile tail.

Even as newly independent pups, they have all the intelligence they will ever have. What's that, you say? Opossum intelligence? Yes, despite their undeserved reputation for stupidity and a brain that is only one-fifth the size of a cat's, opossums are better at remembering where food is hidden than are dogs, cats, or rats.

Opossums are probably most famous for "playing 'possum," that is pretending to be dead when threatened. Actually, as someone who has live-trapped, tagged, and released hundreds of opossums, I can say with some authority that they are much more likely to hiss, growl, and flash those fifty teeth than they are to collapse in a heap and play dead. But for all their bluster, they are surprisingly hesitant to bite. They seldom bite pets and despite handling many, I've never been bitten, although not all my field assistants can say the same.

If this threat doesn't work, they may indeed keel over, drool, excrete foul-smelling goo from their anal glands, and play dead. They will continue to play dead pretty much regardless of what you do to them. Whether they really have fallen into some sort of opossum trance, fainted, or are just pretending, isn't clear. Electronic monitoring of their heart and brain activity shows no differences when they are playing dead compared to when they are normally active, so maybe they are just superb and dedicated actors.

One thing opossums don't have to play dead for is snakes. They are virtually immune to snake venom, thanks to a unique protein in their blood. So copperheads, water moccasins, and even large rattlesnakes are part of the standard opossum diet. Remember this the next time that you aren't bitten by a large rattlesnake. It's the opossum's one form of public service. Eating ticks is another.

Opossums need to get about the business of reproducing quickly, and they can do so as soon as six months of age, because they won't live for long. For reasons that we don't understand they undergo a sort of accelerated aging, so that by the time they are two years old, they begin to show classic signs of aging such as shrinking muscles, a declining immune system, and the development of cataracts. Most wild opossums are actually dead before they reach two years old and of more than one hundred I've put radio collars on and monitored throughout their lives, none has so far lived as long as than three years.

Despite these fascinating traits, opossums will no doubt continue to get little respect. I'm not sure why. They do not carry rabies or other diseases that people need to worry about. With their long snouts, toothy snarl, naked ears and rat-like tail, they certainly fail the "cute" test. Maybe it's no more complicated than that.

The Genius of Fire Ants

I F you live anywhere south of Kentucky and east of New Mexico in the United States, you have probably done a dance I call the fire ant boogie. It doesn't need to be taught. Seconds after you blunder unknowingly through a fire ant mound, which if you live where fire ants live, you *will* do, your ankles suddenly feel like they have burst into flame. You will do the fire ant boogie, trying to shake off your ant tormenters.

I'm sure we have all wondered whether that fire scorching our ankles was due to ant bites or ant stings. The answer is yes. They bite *and* they sting. However, the bite is trivial. You probably didn't even feel it. They bite only to anchor themselves to a bit of skin or a shaft of hair, so that they can then repeatedly stab you with their stinger, each time injecting another load of venom.

Each ant will sting you about half a dozen times in quick succession if she gets a chance. Yes, all those stinging ants are females—sterile female workers. The seldom-seen males are black rather than red and have wings. Stingers evolved from what was originally an egg-laying tube, so you wouldn't really expect males to have them. By the way, be thankful that they sting you so few times. Fire ant workers have enough venom to sting as many as thirty times.

If you stop dancing long enough to look at them closely, you will notice that fire ant females come in many sizes. The largest ones can weigh twenty times as much as the smallest ones. But beware of a small ant's fury. Small ones, it turns out, inject more venom than large ones.

And Southerners quit your whining. According to the Schmidt sting pain scale, fire ant stings are not so bad.

Yes, there really is such a sting pain scale, thanks to entomologist Justin Schmidt. Just as *Consumer Reports* rates cars or refrigerators or weed-whackers, Schmidt rates the painfulness of insect stings. Of course to do this, he must allow himself to be stung by every species he rates, which at last count was well over a hundred and fifty of them. On the Schmidt 0-4 scale, zero is a sting that you hardly feel, two is the sting of a honeybee, and four is the sting of a tarantula hawk wasp or a one-inch tropical bullet ant, which Schmidt describes as "like walking over flaming charcoal with a three inch nail embedded in your heel." The man is a poet of pain.

On the Schmidt scale, fire ant stings rate a relatively mild 1.2. However, that's the rating for only one ant. Fire ants make up for their puny venom with numbers. Most of us get stung by dozens of them at the same time. Not only that, small pustules pop up wherever they stung and those can itch for days.

But I come to praise fire ants, not to bury them with derision about the potency of their stings. If you admire biological sophistication and success, then you have to admire what are now officially named Red Imported Fire Ants or RIFA's for short.

RIFAs may be the most successful invaders since the Vikings. Originally from Argentina and southern Brazil, they have invaded Australia, New Zealand, China, and many islands in the Caribbean as well as North America. As discovered by the famous naturalist, E.O. Wilson, they first came ashore in the U.S. in the early 1930's around Mobile harbor, stowaways in the soil of imported plants. That's right, Alabama for all its other sins can also lay claim to being the beachhead of fire ant invasion on this continent.

Although workers are wingless, fire ants spread by flight. At certain times of the year, colonies produce winged males and females that take to the air in so-called nuptial flights. Having mated once, and only once, while in flight, the females will alight, break off their wings, dig into the soil, and start laying eggs to found a new colony.

From Mobile, they rapidly spread east, north, and west until by the mid-1950's the US Department of Agriculture decided enough was enough. They were causing so much damage to people and property that they needed to be eradicated. In what was basically a carpet bombing campaign throughout the southeast, they employed potent insecticides to try to poison the RIFAs into oblivion. The carnage among pets, livestock, wildlife, and native insects was impressive. After one bout of aerial insecticide bombardment, Monroeville, Alabama hauled more than seven hundred domestic fowl and sixty dog and cat carcasses to the city dump. Nor were livestock spared. And people? No one knows. However, by the time this indiscriminate, poorly conceived, eradication program was halted, fire ants had increased their range by another 50 percent!

This catastrophe caught the attention of marine biologist and nature writer, Rachel Carson, whose 1962 book *Silent Spring* documented the environmental impact of indiscriminate pesticide use. That book is credited with helping launch the modern environmentalism. Who would have guessed that fire ants were indirectly responsible for environmental activism?

So what is the secret of fire ants' success?

One big contributor to their success is people. Fire ants thrive in grassy open areas like parks, pastures, playgrounds, golf courses, and household lawns. Over time, of course, we have created more and more of this prime fire ant real estate. A second contributor is their willingness and ability to eat pretty much anything—dead animals of almost any sort, small defenseless animals of almost any sort, insects, earthworms, seeds, plant sap, you name it. Because they eat almost anything, fire ants can reach stupefying numbers. Each mixing bowl-size mound represents a fire ant colony of roughly two hundred thousand ants. There can be as many as four hundred mounds on the best of fire ant acres. Putting these two things together, it is possible to find as many as eighty million fire ants, which altogether weigh as much as several people, on a single acre.

Fire ant colonies are also particularly adept at surviving flooding. As ground water rises, the workers will hoist their queen and all of the developing larvae aboard a living raft of hundreds of thousands of ants. These ant rafts can float for a couple of weeks if need be and afterwards continue on as a successful colony once the waters recede.

By the way, if you happen upon such an ant raft, avoid it. The colony feels particularly vulnerable when afloat and they sting even more ferociously than usual.

The northerly spread of fire ants appears to be limited by cold. Unusually bad winters in Tennessee, the current northerly limit of their range, kill off a substantial number of colonies. But we all know that unusually harsh winters are becoming more and more rare. Kentucky, Indiana, Illinois, get ready to learn the fire ant boogie.

Chimps in the Kitchen

REMEMBER how irritating it was when after you had spent years mastering some skill, say, throwing a fastball or playing Chopin on the piano, and then one of your siblings decided that he would perfect the same skill just to show you that it was no big deal?

That's a bit like the way I felt when I discovered that chimpanzees had learned to cook.

You might be surprised that I think of chimpanzees as siblings, but in fact they are. We know that because just as DNA can be used to determine how people are related, it can also be used to determine how species are related. Chimpanzees turn out to be our true sibling species, which probably explains why they took so easily to cooking. Chimps are the siblings who stayed home in Africa, where we both started out.

A key question in understanding primate evolution has always been what advantage ancient humans may have had over ancient chimps that allowed us to spread so successfully throughout the world. Harvard primatologist Richard Wrangham has argued that one thing that may have set us apart was our ability to cook.

Did you ever eat a raw potato or raw corn-on-the-cob or a handful of uncooked rice? I would guess the answers might be "yes, tried it once when I was a kid," or "no," or possibly "are you out of your mind?" The reason that we like, or actually need, these things cooked is that cooking alters their chemical structure, making them digestible. They taste good cooked because nature designed our brains quite sensibly to prefer foods from which we can extract lots of nutrients and energy. Energy and nutrients after all are why we eat in the first place.

Once we learned to manage our own fire, probably after thousands of years of running to the sites of wild fires and poking around in the ashes for nutritiously charred roots, fruits, or grain, the world became a much better stocked pantry for us.

To test whether chimpanzees might be capable of at least some of the mental steps required to understand cooking food, scientists devised a fake oven to see if chimps could learn to use it.

We know that chimps are clever, as we expect our relatives to be, but few of us appreciate just how clever. Chimps in the wild use as many as twenty-five different tools, which is roughly twenty-three more than I can use effectively. They also routinely plan for the future. For instance, they might gather nuts which they can't break open by hand, carry the nuts some distance to where there is a very large, flat rock, leave the nuts there while they stomp off in another direction to retrieve a head-size round rock, which they then take back and use to break open the nuts against the flat rock. The longer you watch them, the more amazed you are at their mental skills.

An exceptionally eccentric friend of mine years ago had a pair of chimps as pets because, well, he was exceptionally eccentric. One year his chimps delivered a "chimp-ling" at about the same time that his own daughter had her first baby, his first grandchild. Baby Tino, the chimp not the human, was hand-raised in the house where my friend took great glee in pointing out how much cleverer the chimp baby was than his grand-daughter. Watching them explore (and destroy) the house together, there was no doubt about it. Tiny could run mental circles around the little girl at least up to the age of about two years which is the last time I saw them.

Getting back to cooking. Cooking requires a lot more sophisticated mental steps than you probably have considered. First you have to understand which potential foods can be improved by cooking and which ones can't. This means distinguishing a sweet potato from a sweet potato-shaped piece of wood, for instance. You have to understand, and not eat, your food immediately. You need to let go of it, allow it to disappear into a cooker of some sort for a time, and then understand that later you will get it back, at which time it will be tastier and more edible than before.

This is exactly what chimps have learned to do. Researchers made a fake oven into which they would put a raw sweet potato if the chimp handed it to them. A few minutes later, they would pull a cooked sweet potato out of the oven, and hand it back. The chimps not only learned to do this. They learned not to bother doing so with a sweet potato-shaped piece of wood (which came back still a sweet potato-shaped piece of wood), and they learned not to hand the potato to the other researcher with the other fake oven that never cooked a thing.

We can still feel superior to chimps though, because they haven't mastered fire.

We can't feel the same about speed reading though. Chimps beat us hands down at that. It's as if your sibling took up the piano and in fifteen minutes learned to play better that you could after years of practice.

Ayumu is a male chimpanzee living in a research facility in Japan. Ayumu can beat you, me, and anyone else against whom he has competed, in speed reading.

Here is how it works. *Ayumu* has been taught to count to nine. His speed reading consists of seeing the numbers one through nine appear a random locations on a computer screen for one-fifth of a second. That's less time than it takes you or me to blink. After one-fifth second, the numbers disappear and he has to touch the screen at the places where each had been in the correct numerical order. If he does it, he gets a reward. He gets it right about 90 percent of the time, which turns out to be better than a world-class memory champion, who to his lasting embarrassment competed against *Ayumu*.

So while we may have learned to dominate the earth in ways that our chimpanzee brethren have not, it is not because we were better learners, at least when it comes to cooking and short-term spatial memory.

Pets versus Pests

SOMETIMES we adopt them, sometimes they adopt us.

If we adopt them, it's because we can put them to use. We feed and care for them gladly. We call them pets and adore them. If they adopt us, we call them pests because *they* put *us* to use. We feed and care for them against our will. We do our best to exterminate them. Collies versus cockroaches, in a manner of speaking. Collies—think Lassie—being among our most adored pets, cockroaches being among our most loathed pests.

Which brings us to the mouse, a species with which we have had a long and complicated relationship.

We call virtually any small, furry, long-tailed, pointy-nosed animal a mouse. As a result, there are deer mice, beach mice, grasshopper mice, harvest mice, wood mice, pocket mice, jumping mice, spiny mice, birch mice, dormice, and too many others to mention. But the ones I'm talking about, the one you are most likely to find evidence of in your cupboard, are called, appropriately enough, house mice.

House mice adopted us around ten thousand years ago when humans first developed agriculture in the Middle East, specifically the area now called Iraq. Soon after inventing agriculture, we invented storage bins in which to keep our harvested grain through the winter to guard against famine.

House mice had emerged millions of years earlier on the cold and unpredictable grasslands of central Asia, eking out a living for millennia after millennia foraging for scattered seeds while dodging hawks, snakes, foxes and weasels. Once they discovered humans farming, and learned that just by squeezing through cracks and crevices around our dwellings they could fatten themselves up in relative safety on our stored grain, they saw no reason to ever leave again.

And so they moved in with us uninvited. Being exceptionally well-fed and protected from predators, they multiplied faster than bad news. When times were exceptionally good, their numbers were stupendous. During mouse plagues, a thousand or more mice could swarm around and inside of a single grain silo. Of course, in addition to depleting our food supplies they also had a nasty habit of fouling our storage bins, cupboards, and kitchens with their waste. So from the very beginning, they were the enemy. We were ready and willing to declare war on them. Pests, indeed.

As agriculture spread east and west across Eurasia from Atlantic to Pacific, and north and south from Scandinavia to Sardinia, so did the house mouse. During the Age of Discovery when European mariners sailed to every part of the world, mice sailed along with them. Sailing ships too had everything a mouse could wish for, a cornucopia of stored food plus enough cracks and crannies to hide a small mouse army. When the ships docked, some mice ventured ashore, found more stored food, more hiding places, and more opportunities to get a fresh start in a new life as unwanted and undocumented immigrants.

Today, house mice of Eurasian ancestry have spread to pretty much every part of the world where there are people and a few where there aren't. They have proved to be as adaptable as any animal on earth. They live along the Equator and on subarctic islands. They nest in places as hot as heating ducts and as cold as meat lockers. As part of my research, I have live-trapped mice in fields, farms, hotels, motels, restaurants, and hospitals around the world.

Yes, hospitals. Some of the most successful mouse live-trapping I've ever done was in the sweltering maternity ward of a hospital in Majuro, capital of the tropical Marshall Islands, where the women patients thanked me effusively each morning as I hauled out trapped mice by the dozen.

Along the way, house mice have shifted in size and shape, changed as necessary to adapt to local conditions. In the tropical heat, they shrunk to dwarf size, in the frigid, windy north they grew to be mouse giants. Sometimes they had to abandon their human-based diets altogether. On the Kerguelen Islands in the southern Indian Ocean they eat mainly earthworms. On Gough Island in the south Atlantic, they have been seen mass-attacking and devouring seabird chicks.

Is it any surprise that even now if you could build a better mousetrap, the world would still beat a path to your door?

However, no matter how despised a species is, there always seem to be some people willing to adopt, coddle, selectively breed, and competitively "show" them. The desire to breed-and-show seems to be an even more basic human trait than despising pests. And so in the late 19th century across Eurasia from China to England, there developed "fancy mouse" clubs, where enthusiasts would display their purpose-bred mice with silky or curly or strangely colored fur in order to win ribbons, trophies, or other prizes.

Breeding fancy mice became popular in the United States as well. A retired school teacher named Abbie Lathrop from Granby, Massachusetts turned her hobby into a business, selling loads of her fancy mice to Harvard professor William Castle beginning in 1902. He used the mice and their strange coat colors to investigate new theories of inheritance. They were so useful that he shared the mice with his scientific colleagues who used them for other purposes and before long the laboratory mouse was born. So today's laboratory mice living by the millions in thousands of biological research laboratories around the world descended from fancy mice that were themselves selectively bred from the despised wild house mouse that continues to feed on—and foul—the food in our silos, cupboards, kitchens, and maternity wards on remote islands.

We have at least one other thing to thank these mice for. We weren't the only ones who noticed how they swarmed around our farms and houses. The Eurasian wildcat noticed it as well. If the mice had discovered a life of easy abundance around humans, the wildcats knew they had too.

For many years, it was assumed that what we now call house cats were first domesticated—or maybe more accurately, half-domesticated—from wildcats in Egypt. However recent genetic and archeological evidence points to another place, Iraq, roughly ten thousand years ago. Sound familiar?

A World Without Chocolate?

I MAGINE your worst nightmare. Now think of something worse. Okay, here is something even worse than that. Imagine a world without chocolate!

This thought came to me when I read that *Mars Inc.*, the candy bar maker, had an in-house genetics team examining the genomes of many types of wild and domesticated cacao trees. These are the trees that produce the fruit from which we make chocolate. They were hoping to learn how to make the trees hardier and more disease-resistant.

Yes, chocolate comes from a fruit, a fruit being a plant structure, especially a fleshy structure, containing seeds. So yes, tomatoes are fruit, so are avocados. The reason that plants produce fruits in the first place is to entice animals to eat them and with the help of the animals' digestive system spread their seeds—the next plant generation—far and wide. Of course, if the seeds are chewed up, killed that is, during the fruit eating process, the whole purpose of making fruit is defeated. So nature has wisely designed plants to have tasty flesh but seeds packed with foul tasting or even poisonous chemicals. This makes animals, including human animals, careful about chewing up seeds when they eat fruit. Cyanide, to take one example, is naturally found in the pits, that is, seeds, of apricots, apples, and cherries.

The cacao fruit is no exception. About the size of a beer can, it has a white pulp with a tangy sweet taste and about forty very bitter-tasting seeds due to a chemical called theobromine, a close relative of caffeine. Theobromine, like caffeine, is a poison, although also like caffeine, a poison that in small amounts produces side effects that our brains enjoy. In principle, it is possible to kill yourself by overdosing on chocolate although it is not easy.

For someone my size (pretty average), a steady diet of about seven pounds of dark chocolate per day should do the trick. Dogs as you may know are particularly susceptible to chocolate poisoning. You may not realize that cats are even more susceptible. On the other hand, cats don't have a sweet tooth, so they very sensibly will not gobble a whole box of chocolate candy even if they get the chance.

The first people to domesticate cacao, probably in southeastern Mexico about four thousand years ago, likely figured out that the fruit pulp could be naturally fermented. There is nothing to make people to pay attention to a fruit like discovering that eating it or drinking its juice can make you tipsy. How they figured out that the seeds, or beans as we call seeds of a certain size and shape, could be processed to make chocolate, I'll never understand, because it is both complicated and time consuming.

How complicated and time consuming, you ask? To begin with the fruit must be fully ripe, which meant in those days that you needed to beat the monkeys and the birds to it. Next the seeds need to be separated from the pulp and left to ferment for about a week. This removes much, but not all, of the bitterness. Then the seeds need to be dried quickly before they start to mold in the hot humid tropics. This can take up to another week. Finally, the seeds need to be roasted, the shells removed, and the contents crushed to make a powder from which you can make the food of the gods.

Literally. The scientific name of the cacao tree—okay, let's just call it the chocolate tree—is *Theobroma* (Greek for "food of the gods") *cacao*. Modern chocolate processing is actually much more complicated, although quicker, than this traditional method. But the result is certainly god-like.

Chocolate has had people going bonkers for it for millennia. It was highly valued for religious ceremonies by the Mayans and Aztecs. As chocolate trees would not grow in the mountain valleys where the Aztecs lived, it became so valuable and difficult to obtain that it could be used as money. You could pay your taxes or purchase your dinner with cacao beans. An Aztec turkey would set you back about a hundred beans, an avocado could be had for a measly three beans.

It took Europeans a while to catch on to the wonders of chocolate, but by the 1700's they went crazy for it just as the Aztecs had, and just as virtually everyone else since then. Today fifty million people make a living off of the hundred billion dollar chocolate industry.

Which is why *Mars, Inc.* is investigating the cacao genome. Chocolate trees for centuries have been selectively bred for tastier chocolate, mainly meaning reduced bitterness, but there have been side effects to go along with the selective breeding as there always are. Compared with their wild cousins, modern cacao trees are increasingly finicky. They only grow well in warm, humid areas with plenty of steady rain and not too much wind. Today most commercial chocolate trees are grown in west Africa, relatively close to the equator. Modern trees also don't produce that many fruit. One tree produces only about enough chocolate each year to make about twenty candy bars. And they get a host of diseases, including a fungal disease with possibly the best fungal disease name of all time, frosty pod rot.

The worry is that as the climate changes, these manageable problems will become increasingly unmanageable. Also, unlike most other seeds, cacao seeds will not germinate after being stored for long periods. So banks of stored cacao seeds cannot serve as insurance against environmental catastrophe. Therefore, the hope is that by making use of the genes from the remaining wild cacao stocks, we might be able to genetically modify the chocolate tree to make it more productive, more disease resistant, maybe more able to grow it a variety of climates, and thus more likely to still be with us a century from now.

I don't know about you, but I'm with the Mars folks on this. This is my sort of Mars mission.

Cockroaches Get No Respect
(Even Though They Deserve It)

L ET's be clear right away that a cockroach is nobody's best friend. And yet, even though you may not like them, you have to respect them. At least that's one lesson you could draw from recent studies in which scientists decided to sequence the entire genomes of the two cockroach species found in your house.

One of these, the bigger one, is the misnamed American cockroach—misnamed because they are native to West Africa not America. They arrived here as unintended immigrants along with some of the first European colonists and now they live virtually everywhere from pole to equator. About the length of an AA battery, American cockroaches are urban dwellers, equally at home outside—in garbage cans, dumpsters, and sewers—as inside your kitchen, pantry or favorite restaurant. So the cockroach in your kitchen today may have been skulking through the sewer or dumpster yesterday. This may explain why they are not better liked.

If you need any more reasons not to like them, consider that they will eat virtually anything—bread, leather, paper, fruit, coffee grounds, pet food, *your* food, excrement, rotting wood, rotting leaves, dead skin, dead cockroaches, live cockroaches, hair, even the glue off of book bindings or the stickum on the back of postage stamps. And, yes, what goes in one end comes out the other. What comes out that other end of the cockroach is also something to which many of us are allergic. It—the technical term is frass—mixes nicely with house dust, discarded insect parts, and dust mites to form a fine, airborne, highly allergenic concoction.

I suspect you are still waiting to hear why we should respect cock-roaches. How is this for starters? The American cockroach is a sprinter, able to run up to fifty times their body lengths per second. If they were human size this would translate into a bit over two hundred miles per hour, fast enough to scurry under the fridge before you even think about stomp-ing on them in other words. Also, it turns out that their genome is bigger than ours. Yes, for all of our pride in our big brain and opposable thumbs, American cockroaches in all their sewer-dwelling, allergenic, glue-eating glory have about a thousand genes more than we do. They are particularly well-endowed with genes for taste and smell. No wonder they find many more tastes and smells appealing than we do. More than three hundred of their genes are specialized just for tasting bitter substances. As many poi-sons are bitter, this may be one reason they are so challenging to eliminate. Another reason is that they have a pile of genes that detoxify poisons they might happen to eat.

The Chinese have more respect for American cockroaches than we do. Their Chinese name, *xiao qiang*, means "little mighty," which reminds me of the cartoon character Mighty Mouse. Liquid extract of cockroach is used in traditional Chinese medicine to accelerate the healing of cuts and burns. Fried cockroaches are ground into powder and sold in pill form to treat stomach, liver, and heart diseases.

Like the American cockroach which is not from America, the Ger-man cockroach—the smaller, fingernail size species you are likely to find scuttling about in your kitchen in the dark—is not from Germany. It origi-nated in the jungles of Southeast Asia and is pretty exclusively an indoor pest with a particular fondness for restaurants, hotels, and nursing homes. Actually, in most of the world it is known as the German cockroach, but in Germany itself it is the Russian cockroach. That tells you pretty much all you need to know about the historical relations between Germany and Russia.

German cockroaches share most of the appealing traits of American cockroaches, plus because they are smaller, they can hide in even more places in your restaurant's kitchen. Also, they reproduce faster and are far more numerous than American cockroaches. Next time you find a cock-roach—or worse, half a cockroach—in your soup it will most likely be a German cockroach.

That may sound awful but as long as it is well-cooked to kill the nu-merous bacteria cockroaches carry, you shouldn't worry about it. In many parts of the world people regularly and purposefully dine on cockroaches. Who wants an abundant source of protein to go to waste? In parts of Mexico and Thailand, they are finicky enough to remove the head and legs before sauté-ing, boiling, drying, or dicing them. A little garlic, a little salt, hmmm. In China, cockroaches are actually farmed. Fried twice in a wok of hot oil, they are crispy on the outside, soft on the inside, kind of like cannoli.

German cockroaches have even more genes than American cockroaches—nearly ten thousand more—which means that they have almost 50 percent more genes than you and I do. Those extras taste and smell genes must make the inside of a garbage can into some kind of olfactory symphony to them. It is also somewhat touching how they can recognize their relatives by smell and they help each other find food by leaving an aromatic trail of excrement behind them. Others know to follow that trail, which is why when you find them, you typically find masses of them.

If you're still uncertain as to why scientists would bother to sequence cockroach genomes, it's not to learn about their amazing sprint speed, nor to understand how they can live up to a week after their heads have been removed (the head itself lives only a few hours). No, it is because they are the closest relatives of, and could possibly teach us something about, the origin of—wait for it—possibly the second most reviled insects, termites. Why are scientists particularly interested in termites (hint: it's not pest control)? That's a story for another day.

An Unholy Alliance

Cows, Cane Toads, and Dung Beetles

WHETHER new immigrants are a good or bad thing will depend on who you are and when you are asked.

For instance, if you asked a soil conservation manager during the man-made Dust Bowl environmental catastrophe of the 1930's whether kudzu, an Asian botanical immigrant, was a good thing, he would have told you it was the ideal plant to stabilize your soil and prevent more erosion. In fact, in those days the government would *pay* you to plant kudzu. Kudzu as all Southerners know supports itself by climbing over other plants, trees, buildings, power poles and power lines. Today after kudzu has blanketed and largely destroyed hundreds of thousands of acres of the American southeast and costs millions of dollars a year to control, a soil conservation manager might take a different view. It all goes to show how unpredictable the effects of new biological immigrants can be.

That unpredictability is particularly evident in that epicenter of global environmental catastrophes—Australia. When the first shiploads of convicts, now referred to as "colonists," arrived in England's new penal colony in 1788, they brought with them five cows and two bulls among other barnyard animals. This made a lot of sense as once the bulls and cows got together, their descendants could provide the colony with plentiful meat, milk, and leather. A couple of centuries later there were thirty million cows in Australia and an unexpected problem had emerged—cow pies, a.k.a cow pats, or cow dung. Whatever you call them, Australia was gradually being buried under them.

Among the earth's unsung environmental heroes are dung beetles. Ancient Egyptians realized this and made one species of dung beetle, the scarab, sacred. Dung beetles as the name implies eat, bury, lay eggs, and brood their young in dung. Consequently, they are largely responsible for disposing of the earth's dung, recycling its components, aerating and enriching the soil at the same time.

Prior to the arrival of cows, Australia had been isolated from other continents for about one hundred million years, evolving its own specialized plants and animals. Australian dung beetles were adept at disposing of kangaroo and wombat dung which is hard, dry, and fibrous, but not at processing moister, softer, flatter cow dung. Without the right beetles, cow dung accumulated. Doing the math, thirty million cows, roughly twelve cow pats per cow each day, and about six million acres of Australian pasture land was being buried under cow dung each year. Not only that, Australian flies, some of which were fierce and painful biters, were finding they could breed enthusiastically in that stuff.

To the rescue came beetle-and-dung biologists. They noticed that Africa with its millions upon millions of hoofed cow relatives had no dung problem, so maybe African dung beetles were the answer to Australia's problem? Taking no chances are transmitting African cattle diseases, the scientists carefully picked beetle eggs from African cattle dung, sterilized them chemically, and pushed them lovingly into sterilized Australian cattle dung (who says science isn't glamorous?). After years of careful study, they released the first African dung beetles along the northern Australia coast in 1967 and hoped for the best.

It worked.

Pastures were rapidly cleared of dung and biting fly numbers plummeted. Within two years the beetles had spread more than two hundred fifty miles along the coast and fifty miles inland. Today, Australia is the second largest beef exporter (behind Brazil) in the world thanks to this classic case of successful biological control.

All medicines have side effects though. One of the side effects of importing African dung beetles was an explosion in Australia's population of cane toads, another immigrant. Cane toads, native to south and central America, are huge. Some are the size of baseball mitts, and weigh up to four pounds. Toads of this size are not fleet or agile. They protect themselves with a deadly poison secreted from glands on top of their head. One toad contains enough poison to kill a large crocodile.

Cane toads were deliberately introduced into Australia in 1935 in the hope that they would control beetles that were devastating Australia's sugar cane. This introduction wasn't done with the care and forethought of the dung beetle introduction. For one thing, the cane beetles were active during the day, the cane toads were active mainly at night. For another, the cane beetles hung out at the top of the sugar cane plants whereas the toads were earthbound, too big to climb much of anything.

Dung beetles on the other hand were nocturnal like the toads and hung out on the ground, on cow pats specifically. Cane toads soon learned that if they headed for the nearest dung pat around dusk, beetles would soon be arriving in droves. Toads gobbled the beetles like so much sushi. A single toad could eat more than a hundred of them in one sitting.

Cane toads were soon at plague proportions. This was problematic as they were lethal to anything that tried to eat them, whether it was native Australian predators or pet dogs and cats. There was worry among conservationists that toad poisoning would eventually lead to the extinction of numerous predatory native species not to mention native toads.

They also became a nuisance simply because of their overwhelming abundance. So many were flattened by cars, that roads at certain times of the year almost seemed to be paved in toads. Efforts at control failed, so the Australians responded as Australians will by turning them into practical amusement, inventing their own control strategies. They invented cane toad golf, cane toad cricket, and cane toad pitching contests (the road-flattened toads make passable Frisbees). Cane toads were turned into purses, ash trays, and wall-mounted souvenirs. Cane toad licking became a cheap high among Australian teenagers—small doses of their toxin gave a similar high to LSD from all reports. Cane toads became the state icon of Queensland.

As I say, the environmental effects of immigration are unpredictable and whether they are good or bad depends on who you ask and when you ask. To an Australian cattle rancher, dung beetles saved their industry. To conservationists, they are a threat to native wildlife because of the explosion of toads they cause. To a cane toad, they are just dinner.

Immigrants You Can't Live Without

WE all know the story of undocumented immigrants. You admit a few because they are willing to perform menial chores that the locals can't, or won't, do. They do their jobs so well that demand for their services grows. Eventually they become indispensable. They settle down, have a bunch of kids, and by then you can't get rid of them without destroying the economy. I'm talking, of course, about honey bees.

It's easy to forget that honey bees—not to be confused with bumble bees, carpenter bees, or sweat bees—are about as American as the Union Jack and warm beer. Called white-man's flies by native Americans, honey bees were dragged along to the New World by some of our first uninvited immigrants, British colonists, to provide wax and honey. In the seventeenth century honey was the one reliably available sweetener. It was more than a century before farmers figured out that many of their crops did much better when honey bees were around. Insect pollination was discovered.

Honey bees followed the settlers west, arriving in Utah with the Mormons in 1848. Five years later, they arrived in California. Today California agriculture would be crippled without them. They pollinate commercial apricots, blueberries, cherries, cucumbers, pears, watermelons, alfalfa, asparagus, broccoli, Brussels sprouts, cabbage, carrots, clover, and radishes. They also pollinate almonds. California produces 80 percent of the world's almonds. During the almond growing season, 60 percent of the United States' commercial bee hives—more than 1.5 million of them—are transported to California to pollinate the almonds. The value of honey bee pollination services in the United States has been estimated as high as ten billion dollars annually. All the crops I mentioned, by the way, are also uninvited immigrants to the New World. Honey bees, you might say, are as American as apple pie—apples having been introduced to the New World by British colonists at about the same time as honey bees.

There is now a growing worry among farmers that honey bees, those foreign invaders, are slowly vanishing. Colony collapse disorder, as it is called, killed about half of all hives in the United States during the winter of 2012-2013. No one is exactly sure what causes this disorder although the use of some types of pesticide and a recent invasion by a new bee parasite appear to be contributing to it. Ironically, even the greenest environmentalists are now calling for urgent preservation measures for this introduced species, because honey bees have displaced so many native bees that there is now worry that without them there would not be enough pollinators to ensure that some of our native wildflowers can survive.

The point of this discussion of honey bees is to point out how reliant we are not just on human immigrants but on plant and animal immigrants as well. If we could be magically transported back to 1491 just before Columbus' arrival, the American landscape would be virtually unrecognizable. No dandelions, yarrow, Queen Anne's lace, sweet clover, or hundreds of other roadside wildflowers. The eastern forests are dominated by the majestic American chestnut, a tree that has now virtually disappeared thanks to another uninvited immigrant, the chestnut blight fungus. On the west coast, you'd find no orange or lemon groves. The mythic Old West owes a lot to the Old World too. Without Old World immigrants, we'd have no horses, no cattle. Rugged individualists heading west might be wrangling herds of buffalo, riding—what?—antelopes instead? No pigs wallowing, or chickens squawking, in the barnyard. No sheep to start skirmishes between homesteaders and cattle—oops, buffalo—men. No tumbling tumbleweeds (more properly, Russian thistle, introduced into the Dakotas in 1873 in a shipment of Russian flax).

What would household life be like without imported house mice, German cockroaches, and introduced fruit flies buzzing around the bananas (another immigrant)? The mice could have their way because there were also no domestic cats and you couldn't get your morning giddyup because tea and coffee were only found in the Old World. European colonists in America had to wait nearly a century for a Frenchman, Gabriel de Clieu, to introduce coffee to the New World

Not all immigrants became indispensable. Some we'd like very much to dispense with, if we could. These are mostly immigrants that are too small to be visible to the naked eye. I'm talking flu, measles, yellow fever, and of course recently the AIDS, West Nile, Ebola, and COVID-19 viruses, not to mention bacteria that cause tuberculosis, plague, typhus, whooping cough, and typhoid. By some estimates, immigrant diseases killed off over 90 percent of native Americans before Europeans had fully explored the country.

So the next time you hear someone glibly describe the United States as a land of immigrants, maybe you should pause a moment to consider how thoroughly that description is true.

The Nuclear (as in Bomb) Family

PHILANDERING, infidelity, fooling around, whatever you call it, is always in the news. It can cause chaos in otherwise happy families. Yet it seems we hear about it more and more. Where have our morals gone?

I'm talking, of course, about bluebirds.

For people who like to draw lessons from nature, birds may at first glance appear to be exemplars of family values. Unlike most mammals in which males mate and immediately get out of town, birds typically form monogamous pairs. Both parents work hard building their nest. They share the job of feeding and protecting their young. Some species mate for life.

Or so we thought.

The demise of this Disney-fied view of bird life began several decades ago when scientists, suspecting that there might be more to the family life of birds than meets the eye, vasectomized some male blackbirds only to discover that their supposedly monogamous mates continued to lay fertile eggs and raise perfectly normal broods of young.

Something strange was going on.

Then came the news about bluebirds. It wasn't enough that the male's song turned out not to be not so much an expression of springtime joy but more like an bird version of look-at-me chest thumping or engine revving, it also turned out that for all their aggressive posturing, bluebird males had often been duped by their mates. Genetic testing by inquisitive biologists proved that some eggs their mates had been laying were actually fathered by other males. Sometimes the real father was a neighbor. Sometimes, he was a complete stranger.

Oblivious to their non-paternity, the males worked hard to feed and protect all the eggs and young anyway. Would they still do so if they knew?

Yes, mom had been caught stepping out. And because for every philanderer, there has to be a philanderee, dads had to be stepping out too. Bluebirds apparently are not the paragon of family values that we might have imagined.

Then something similar was found in swans, the supposed purest example of mate-for-life-dom. Then it was found in eagles, in herons, in one species after another. Even beavers, one of the rare mammals that reputedly mated for life because they worked so hard together building and remodeling their living quarters, were found to have at least two fathers in half of their litters. What was the world coming to?

Bird researchers had to invent a whole new vocabulary to cover what humans might call the misdeeds that birds were found to routinely commit. The bloodless but nonjudgmental technical term for "stepping out" became having "extra-pair copulations" or EPCs. Simple "monogamy" gave way to "social monogamy" which means the nest-building couple work together to raise the brood, as if they were the biological parents even if they may not be.

Philandering turns out not to be the worst thing (from our human perspective) that birds do—not by a long shot.

Remember the movie *The March of the Penguins*? It was a surprise 2005 hit documentary about the incredible bond between Emperor penguin parents and physical hardship they endured to raise their single chick during the Antarctic winter and how that bond, strengthened by adversity, survived year after year until death did them part?

That bond and hardship were very real.

After an arduous several week-long trek from the ocean over pack ice to the breeding colony, Emperors pair up, the female lays a single egg which she passes to her mate, where upon she immediately heads back to the sea to feed and restore her energy reserves. Males warm and protect that egg during the coldest and windiest season of the coldest windiest continent on earth. By the time the female returns and finds her mate again among thousands of penguins, he will not have eaten for four months. He may have lost more than half of his body weight. Yet he has faithfully held on to that egg, and if it hatched, the chick. She then takes over the chick's care, allowing her mate to return to the sea to restore his own energy reserves.

They alternate care this way until the chick can eventually march to the sea and feed itself.

That's what happens if everything goes right.

But it's the Antarctic winter and things often do not go right. If the female returns and her chick is dead or missing, because her mate has accidently dropped the egg or abandoned it rather than starve to death, she will often try to kidnap a chick from another parent. You might call this a kind of adoption rather than a kidnapping except that even if she is successful, she soon loses interest in the stolen, unrelated chick and abandons it to die on the ice.

Oh, and the "mate for life" thing of Emperor penguins turns out most often to be "mate for the season," then find a new mate next year—the Henry VIII model of monogamy.

So probably the safest lesson in morality to be learned from these sordid little tales of bird life would be not to draw moral lessons from nature in the first place. If you insist though, there does seem to be at least one well-confirmed case of long-term monogamy you can take to heart—the pork tapeworm, a species we should all hope to emulate.

Dinosaurs in the Garden

I F you still think that all the dinosaurs were killed off some sixty-five million years ago when that massive asteroid crashed into the earth extinguishing three-quarters of all plant and animal species, you are mistaken. One group of dinosaurs survived. They are related to *Tyrannosaurus rex* and *Velociraptor*, those agile and eerily clever predators made famous by the *Jurassic Park* movies. You might be able to hear some of these modern dinosaurs singing melodiously in the garden right now. We call them birds.

Modern paleontologists often refer to those extinct dinosaurs as non-avian—that is, non-bird—dinosaurs to distinguish them from avian dinosaurs, the ones with feathers that fly and yodel in the spring. Once you begin to look for it, their similarity to traditional dinosaurs becomes striking.

Two similarities in particular stand out. *Velociraptor* and its relatives, like very few other animals ever to roam the earth, walked on two hind limbs or, as we call them, legs. All birds do the same thing and have done so since their origin in the middle of the Age of Dinosaurs. Also, all birds, and no other living animals, have feathers. The only other creatures that also had feathers were dinosaurs. Whether the feathered dinosaurs flew or not is still up in the air, so to speak.

Feathers, of course, are one of nature's most spectacular inventions. They are a unique combination of light weight, strength, flexibility, and adaptability. Some, like wing feathers, are shaped and stiffened for aerodynamic purposes, others have remarkable waterproofing ability, still others, down feathers, are soft with exceptional insulating properties. Humans, of

119

course, have taken advantage of feathers' exquisite insulating properties in down blankets and parkas and their softness in pillows, comforters, and mattresses. Feathers also come in all the colors of the rainbow and an endless variety of color patterns. Think Cardinal, Bluebird, Peacock.

Why would dinosaurs have evolved feathers before they evolved flight? Probably because of feathers' exquisite ability to trap heat. Insulation from their feathers helps birds retain body heat and probably did the same for dinosaurs, a number of which are now thought to have been warm-blooded.

We shouldn't forget the missing link that ties everything together. Discovered in southern Germany in 1861, just two years after Darwin published *On the Origin of Species*, *Archaeopteryx* was the spitting image of a crow-size *Velociraptor*. It had *Velociraptor* teeth and a long bony *Velociraptor* tail. It even had *Velociraptor*-like claws on its forelimbs and that large scimitar of a killing claw on its feet. It also had wings and feathers. *Archaeopteryx* may be our best example of nature caught in transition between one form and another.

It is time to burst a few movie-goer bubbles. *Velociraptor* in real life was turkey size, much smaller than the movie version. Second—*Jurassic Park* fans close your ears—they had feathers. I know that spoils their fearsome image at bit, but I'm willing to give Steven Spielberg a break on the biological realism because the first Jurassic Park movie came out fourteen years before scientists discovered that *Velociraptors* were feathered.

Birds may be dinosaurs but they required some specialized changes from other dinosaurs if they were to master flight. And master it they did. Today, they fly higher, faster, farther, as well as flip, dip, and dive with more agility, than any other flying animals living or dead. Common garden birds perform spectacular acrobatics so routinely that we seldom notice -- for instance, braking in a split second from their thirty mile per hour cruising speed to land precisely poised on pencil-thin branches.

To succeed in the air, they needed to lose some weight. The less a flying animal weighs relative to size of its wings and the power of its muscles, the more quickly and easily it can take off and the longer it can remain aloft. To reduce weight birds, compared with their dinosaur kin, reduced the size of some bones, made others hollow, and lost a few altogether. They replaced the long bony dinosaur tail with a light but sturdy fan of tail feathers. They replaced the heavy tooth-lined dinosaur jaw with a light toothless beak.

Birds reduced weight in less obvious ways too. They lack urinary bladders, for instance, minimizing the liquid waste they carry with them and except during breeding, their reproductive organs are vanishingly tiny. Birds are also light because much of their insides are filled with air due to extensive space-filling air sacs which are part of their exceptionally efficient respiratory system.

Yes, birds have come a long way since they were tiny, feathered, flying *Velociraptors*. However, every once in a while that old inner raptor emerges. Consider my normally placid pet chicken, Penny, from many years ago. Penny spent most of the day dozing in her nest box. However, if a lizard made the mistake of venturing on to her territory, Penny would snap awake like Dracula at midnight and do her best *Velociraptor* imitation. Chasing it down with grim efficiency, she would flip the lizard into the air, catch it in her beak, and slam the unfortunate creature repeatedly against the ground—tenderizing it, I suspect. After a quick meal, she would settle back into her roost, close her eyes, and no doubt begin to dream about her *Velociraptor* past.

Some Grass, Man?

NATURE abhors lawns, if by "lawns" you mean uniform patches of mown and manicured grass.

If you don't believe me, put away the mower, the fertilizer, the herbicide, the water hose, and watch what happens.

Soon your lawn will be having sex. Yes, lawn mowing keeps grass in a permanent state of adolescence. Once you allow it to grow beyond its normal mown length though, it will begin producing flowers. You have to look closely to notice them, but those tiny spike-like things that grow on the tips of unmown grass are flowers, or plant genitalia as we biologists like to think of them.

The wind disperses grass pollen, some of which will fall on the female parts of grass flowers and soon you have little grass babies—seeds, in other words.

Without the mower chopping them back to stumps, your lawn will sprout what lawn-lovers call weeds, what the rest of us call wild flowers. Eventually, you have a meadow.

Nature may abhor lawns but people adore them. So much so that if you put together all the lawns in the U.S., including the parks, the parkways, the golf courses, the cemeteries, the football, soccer, and baseball fields, it totals as much acreage as the state of Texas.

Because we have to continually fight nature to preserve our lawns, they cost a bundle. Lawn care is an eighty billion dollar industry. We spend four billion dollars per year just purchasing new lawn mowers. And we *spill(!)* more gasoline each year when sloppily re-fueling those lawn mowers than the Exxon Valdez spilled into Prince William Sound, Alaska in the spring of 1989.

Also, because we've been brain washed into believing that lawns should be nice and green, even in the winter when grass wants to go brown and rest, we now spray nine billion gallons of water on our lawns daily. In case you're keeping track, that's almost three hundred gallons of water each day for every man, woman, and child in America. Any wonder that when there is a drought, limiting lawn watering is the first course of action?

We dump millions of *pounds* of pesticides and herbicides and millions of *tons* of fertilizer on our lawns too. Then it rains and these chemicals flow into our lakes, streams, and ultimately into our drinking water.

So the cost of lawns is both financial and environmental. Not to mention the time we spend on them.

Then there is the immigration problem. Virtually all American lawns are made of grasses native to somewhere else. Bermuda grass is not from Bermuda. It's from Africa. Kentucky bluegrass is not from Kentucky. It's from Europe. Together these two invaders make up the majority of lawns, parks, and playing fields in America.

All of which brings up the question of why we find lawns so attractive in the first place.

Even I, a confirmed hater of any form of yard work, find a large expanse of mown and maniacally manicured lawn like, say, a professional baseball field, delightful to see.

One idea is that a lawn resembles a well-grazed savanna. When our distant primate ancestors decided to move out of the African forest and head into open country, a well-grazed savanna meant there were abundant animals to hunt. It also meant that if you stood upright, you could see approaching lions from a long way off. Is our love of lawns an ancient instinct?

Lawns also resemble well-grazed pastures. In fact the direct ancestor of American lawns was probably the British village green, a common grassy area set aside for communal grazing of livestock. Of course, prior to the invention of the lawnmower, grazing was pretty much the only way you could get a large field of short grass. The alternative was to whack it with a scythe. An even better alternative was to have your servants whack it with scythes. Which is why the first lawns planted solely for pleasure and beauty belonged to the aristocracy. They could afford the scythe-whacking servants. They could also afford to own land and not use it for growing food. Maintaining a large, well-managed lawn was an advertisement of wealth.

It's difficult to imagine that so many of us love lawns because they are a symbol of someone else's wealth though.

Lawns were democratized by the invention of the lawn mower. Despite that, the residential lawn, the pride of American middle-class suburban life and the bane of yard work haters like me, needed two more developments before it could really take off.

First was standardization of the five day, forty hour work week. That was legislated by Congress in 1940 and it freed up Saturdays for slaving in your yard rather than for your employer.

Second was the spread of the of the mass-produced, cookie-cutter suburbs, in which each house had its own small lawn. We can thank Bill Levitt for that. In fact, the lawn care industry ought to build a giant monument to Bill Levitt. *Time* magazine named him "one of the hundred most influential people of the 20th century" for his invention of cheap suburban housing or Levitt-towns, as his early developments were called. A GI returning from World War II could purchase one of Bill's houses for as little as four hundred dollars upfront money and that house included kitchen appliances, a television, and a pre-planted lawn. Part of the deal, if you read the fine print though, was that you had to mow your lawn at least once a week between April 15th and November 15th.

There would be no sex among the grasses of Levitt-towns.

Not surprisingly, Bill's dad considered lawn maintenance a badge of good character. "A fine carpet of green grass stamps the inhabitants as good neighbors, as desirable citizens," as he put it.

I guess I must be a non-desirable citizen then, because I've watched with secret glee as my own lawn withered and wilted during a recent drought. I've learned that what I really crave is a "Freedom Lawn." A Freedom Lawn, the name comes from either "freedom from work" or maybe from "freedom from the enforced conformity of lawn culture," is really an anti-lawn. Invented—or should I say, re-discovered—by some Yale professors in the 1990's, a freedom lawn is a lawn that is pretty much left to its own devices. You don't water it or put any chemicals on it. You can mow it, but only with a push mower. In the end, you waste no water and add no pollutants to your local streams or fossil fuel residue to the atmosphere. You just sit back and watch the dandelions and the clovers and the chickweeds and the violets take over.

So I think I've discovered why *I* like lawns anyway. They are a symbol of hard, honest, physical labor. And I adore hard, honest, physical labor, as long as someone else is doing it. Which makes the best place to get my manicured lawn fix when I need it—the baseball park, where *they* do the all the work.

Octopuses, Octopi, Whatever

OCTOPI? Octopuses? Octopodes? Whatever you call them (octopodes is the least used but most linguistically correct term), they are among the strangest looking and most eerily intelligent animals on the planet, more intelligent in some ways than children. If treated well, they can be friendly, even playful. You might imagine they would make interesting pets. In fact, they do not, for reasons that may surprise you.

Appearing like something dreamed up by a hallucinatory science fiction writer—eight snakes emerging from a floppy hat with eyes—when you look at an octopus, it is likely to look, really look, back. It is easy to get the rather disconcerting feeling when staring deeply into their eyes, that there is someone at home in there and that someone is sizing you up.

Octopuses, to go with the more traditional plural form, do seem to size people up. Some they will give a multi-armed caress, others they will squirt with seawater any chance they get. They may go months without seeing someone, but still remember that person and also remember whether he deserved a squirt or a cuddle.

What octopuses actually see is a bit of a mystery. Biologists who have dissected octopus eyes, examined them at great length under microscopes, peered deeply into their genome, are convinced that they cannot see color. None of the standard color-distinguishing eye pigments can be found. Yet octopuses have a talent for changing color and pattern to match their background that puts chameleons to shame. How they do that without color vision is one of their more enduring mysteries.

They are also excellent problem solvers. Because they get bored in captivity, shuffling aimlessly back and forth, aquarists have a history of providing octopuses with toys. Consequently, we know that they can learn to open and close child-proof pill bottles, something with which many of us adults struggle. One researcher designed the ultimate octopus toy, a series of three Plexiglas boxes fitted inside one another. In the innermost box was a small food reward, a crab. To get to the crab, you had to open two latches on the outermost box, then open a different type of latch on the second box, and open yet a third type of latch on the inner most box. Octopuses had no trouble learning to do this.

Which brings us to why octopuses don't make good pets.

First, they are escape artists and don't hesitate to leave their tanks if sufficiently motivated. Strong enough to lift many aquarium lids, they can ooze through surprisingly small cracks and fissures and end up in places they really don't belong like your closet or teapot. In a case worthy of Sherlock Holmes, fish began disappearing from a public aquarium tank in Brighton, England. The case was solved only when the octopus who had learned to leave its tank at night, crawl into to the fish tank, eat its fill, and return home before morning, was discovered asleep one morning still inside the fish tank. Knowing that your pet octopus might be roaming the house at night, perhaps giving you an unexpected caress in your sleep, could make sleep itself a bit difficult.

The other reason octopuses don't make good pets is that for all their intelligence and endearing personalities, they are surprisingly short-lived. People become attached to their pets and having them age and die within in a year or two, as most octopus do, would be traumatic. Even the giant Pacific octopus which can weigh more than one hundred pounds with a seven foot arm span, only lives about three years.

Like salmon and century plants, octopuses begin aging dramatically soon after the octopus equivalent of puberty. They stop eating and lose the ability to coordinate movement of those eight arms. They also lose the ability solve problems or heal wounds if they are injured. Without eating, they gradually waste away, losing up to half of their muscle mass. The loss of muscle makes their eyes even more prominent, so that they are disturbingly reminiscent of starving children. Within a couple of months they die.

So stick with the dogs, cats, snakes, and parakeets. They may not be as smart or as personable as octopuses, but at least they will be with you for a while.

The Puzzle of Sex

I 'M pretty sure that we biologists think a lot differently about sex than the rest of the world. For one thing, we're puzzled by the fact that it—sex—exists in the first place. For another, we're stumped by why two sexes seem to be just the right number. Why not three? Or five?

Let's be clear. By "sex" I mean the strange fact that for most species, it takes two very different individuals to reproduce. One sex, the male, makes vast numbers of tiny, highly mobile reproductive cells called sperm. The other produces fewer, much larger, reproductive cells packed with nutrients for the developing embryo. We call these eggs, and the individuals that produce them, females. Reproduction by sex requires the uniting of a male's sperm and a female's egg. That's Biology 101.

What is puzzling about sex is that it seems so inefficient. Why should it require two individuals to reproduce? If any single individual could produce offspring by herself, then a population of such individuals could pump out twice as many offspring as a population divided into males and females. In fact, a few species do this. One example is the whiptail lizard, the state reptile of New Mexico. No males of this species have ever been found. Females produce eggs that spontaneously develop into new females. Strangely enough, in order for their eggs to begin developing, two females must go through simulated mating with one another.

But all-female species like the whiptails are vanishingly rare in nature. So reproduction involving both males and females must have some big advantage. One possibility is that sex creates genetic diversity and diversity itself has big advantages, such as allowing species to adapt to changing conditions. In an all-female species each mother can produce only daughters genetically identical to herself. Sex changes that. Each sexually-produced offspring will be genetically unique, a random selection of genes from the father mixed with those from the mother. The cost of this diversity, though, is that it takes two individuals to make one new one.

Some species try to have the best of both worlds. Take the pea aphid, for instance, everyone's favorite plant pest. For most of the year, there are only female pea aphids producing new all-daughter generations about once a month. However as winter approaches, they shift course and produce a single generation of males and females. After mating, which increases genetic diversity as sex always does, the aphids return to producing all-female generations for the next year.

Another way that nature tries to get round the inefficiency of having two separate sexes is by having single individuals that contain both sexes—hermaphrodites, as they are called. Earthworms, for instance, have both male and female reproductive parts. When two earthworms mate, sperm from one fertilizes eggs from the other and vice versa. Each worm ends up as both mother and father to the resulting worm-lings.

While earthworms are *simultaneously* male and female, other species do it sequentially. For instance, in the movie *Finding Nemo*, Nemo, a clownfish, becomes separated from his father, Marlin, after his mother is eaten by a barracuda. Most of the movie consists of Marlin looking for his lost son. This may come as a shock, but in real clownfish, when an adult female, who is the biggest fish in those small social groups living on sea anemones, disappears, the adult male in the group transforms into a female. In real life in other words, Marlin would have transformed into Marilyn as he, I mean she, looked for his, I mean her, son. In some other fishes, sex change goes in the opposite direction. In these cases, males are the larger sex. They defend both a territory and a harem of smaller females. If something happens to the territorial male, the largest harem female will transform into a new territory-defending male.

And then, of course, there is the blue-banded goby, a small fish that can change sexes repeatedly, and in both directions, depending on the social situation.

Most animals cannot change sex. But the way some species end up as either males or females can be pretty unusual. For instance, unlike humans or cows or cats in which sex is determined genetically, the sex of most turtles is determined by temperature. Eggs incubated at one temperature hatch out as all males. At other temperatures, as all females, and at still others you get a mix of sexes. Crocodiles and alligators also use temperature to determine what sex they will be.

And then there is the green spoonworm, a finger-length worm with a long feeding arm that pokes and prods for food on the ocean floor. Actually, that describes the *female* green spoonworm. The male is tiny. It weighs less than one-thousandth as much as the female, cannot feed on his own, and spends most of his life as a parasite living inside the female reproductive tract. You might think this would be a sad, lonely life for a spoonworm male but you would be wrong. As many as eighty-five males have been found living inside a single female. Even stranger is the way that sex is determined. Spoonworm larvae float in the sea as neither male nor female. When they finally settle on to the sea floor, they grow into females. On the other hand, if they happen to settle on top of a female (they are chemically attracted to nearby females), they develop into mini-males, crawl inside the female and spend the rest of their lives in the company of other males, comfortably fertilizing that female's eggs.

As I said at the beginning, biologists think about sex a lot differently than most people. And there are plenty of different kinds of sex in the natural world to think about. At the very least, I hope that the next time you hear someone describe some human behavior as "unnatural," you might tell them about Nemo's father or the green spoonworm.

The Worldwide (Spider) Web

I'M afflicted with web aversion. In all likelihood, so are you. I'm not talking about distaste for the internet. I'm talking about our instinct to recoil when we blunder into a spider's web, particularly a web at face level.

A California professor proved it. He rigged a wooden frame so that his pet orb-weaving spider, the kind that builds flat webs that look something like archery targets, would build a web across the doorway to his office. He then recorded the reactions of students as they blithely walked through the door to see him and got a face-full of spider web. He couldn't help chuckling when telling me that he never saw a single student who didn't recoil. More often than not, they did something much more dramatic than that. I forgot to ask him how many students ever visited his office twice.

It's too bad that most people have this aversion. Spider silk is one of nature's wonders which we ought to appreciate. For its weight, it is stronger than steel, more elastic than nylon. Spiders may not have invented silk. Some insects, silk moths for instance, produce it too. Spiders, however, perfected it and incorporated it into every aspect of their lives.

People are most familiar with spider silk as it's used in webs to capture prey, but there are some bizarre variations on this theme. My favorite is the bolas spider. They hunt for moths at night by dangling a single strand of silk which has a blob of stickum on the end—something like fishermen with bait and a hook on the end of the line. This analogy is more than a casual one as these spiders bait their line with chemicals that mimic the pheromones that female moths use to attract males. Some species of bolas spiders can even shift the chemicals they emit to match the types of moths that happen to be in the vicinity that night. If the fish ain't biting, change bait. If the fish still ain't biting, bolas spiders, unlike most fishermen, finally give up and eat the bait themselves.

Some spiders like those large black and yellow garden spiders you see in the summer leave their webs in place all the time and repair them only as needed. Other species, particularly those that hunt at night, build their webs at dusk then eat them again in the morning—an early silk recycling program. It used to be thought that this habit was only a way to recycle silk proteins but it has now been discovered that spiders get additional nutrition from wind-dispersing pollen grains that are blown into the web's sticky strands.

Spiders produce at least seven different kinds of silk. Web building is only one of its many uses. Small spiders use silk to fly. They climb to an exposed perch, point their abdomens skyward, extrude a few long strands of very light silk, and get hoisted away by the wind like hang gliders plunging off a cliff. Some of their flights are extraordinary. They occasionally are hoisted high enough to reach the jet stream. Spiders have been found to travel hundreds of miles like this, consequently they have colonized the most remote islands on earth.

Spiders also use silk to protect their young. Clutches of eggs are deposited in a silken egg sac. In some species the egg sac is itself protected inside a nursery web on which the mother stands guard. A green lynx spider while guarding its young this way will squirt venom almost a foot if she feels threatened—mother love at its most vivid.

Spiders trail silk behind themselves no matter where they go. Called a dragline, this silk is used like mountaineers use pitons and ropes, to anchor themselves in case they fall and allow them to re-trace their steps if need be. If you want a rough idea of how many spiders live in your house take a look at the cobwebs that accumulate on your walls and window sills. These are mostly draglines left behind by spiders as they walk around your house as you sleep.

Adult males of web-building species don't themselves build webs. They give it up when they become adults. They also eat little if anything. Their lives are reduced to exquisite simplicity. All they do is search for mates. They still use silk though—to make draglines and sperm webs. Spider mating is a complex affair and not just because females may not hesitate to dine on her mate once she has had her way with him. Before mating, male spiders must make a small web on which they deposit sperm which they then suck into bulbs at the end of the tiny leg-like appendages, called pedipalps, near their mouths. Pedipalps are male spiders' mating appendages. You can distinguish adult males from female spiders of any species by noting whether they have a tiny bulb at the end of their pedipalps or not.

I haven't begun to exhaust the ways that spiders use silk, but I feel obligated to at least mention a few human uses. In some places without modern medicine spider silk is used to bind wounds. Silk of large golden silk spiders is used to make fishing nets in some cultures. If you've ever stumbled into the enormous web of one of these harmless spiders, you won't forget it. The silk is noticeably stronger than that of other species. You can hang your sunglasses (as I have done) on a strand of this silk. That same silk is now being used experimentally in human surgery to suture wounds, form tissue support meshes, and to guide regenerating nerves.

My favorite use of this tough golden silk though is to make violin strings. This has been a pet project of Japanese researcher Shigeyoshi Osaki for years. Alas, it will never be a commercially viable material considering that the thickest violin string requires fifteen thousand strands of silk, which takes a lot of time and a lot of spiders to obtain. On the other hand, you could probably dangle a locomotive from this G-string. Dr. Osaki claims that the sound is "brilliant." Of course, he is likely to be biased. Snippets of Tchaikovsky's music played on a Stradivarius violin with either nylon, steel, or spider silk strings can be found on—what else?— the worldwide web.

Ticks and Mosquitoes Suck

INQUIRING minds might wonder which of nature's many blood-sucking parasites is the most revolting. (Insert your own politician joke here). No, I'm talking about animals that literally suck blood for a living—mosquitoes and ticks may come to mind first, but don't forget fleas, lice, and leeches. Vampire bats are disqualified because don't suck. They slice-and-lap your blood like dogs lap water out of a bowl.

I find ticks the most repulsive, but that may just be personal taste. However, if I were a disease-causing organism like, say, a Zika or Dengue fever virus, that lives inside blood suckers and depends on them to reproduce—that is, infect new suckees—I would no doubt prefer to live inside mosquitoes.

The problem with ticks from a disease virus's perspective is that they are slow, infrequent, indiscriminate eaters. True, ticks have the advantage that they only suck blood and never eat anything else, whereas mosquitoes will also dine on flower nectar or other plant juices. But common ticks, like those you find on yourself or your dog after a nice summer's day walk in the woods, eat only three times in their entire lives and they take their time about it.

The common tick life cycle is to hatch from the egg as a pristine larval tick, carrying no diseases. You'd recognize a larval tick. It looks very much like an adult tick, squat and flat, except that it's much smaller and has six rather than the standard eight legs. The larval deer tick, for instance, the species that is infamous for transmitting Lyme disease, is about the size of the period at the end of this sentence. Adults are about the size of an apple seed.

Ticks find their hosts, or victims, as I think of them, by questing. That is in fact the technical term, which I know sounds more like something Sir Lancelot rather than a tick should be doing, but all it means is climbing on to the tip of some vegetation and waiting around, hoping to grasp on to a passing host that brushes against the vegetation. Most ticks aren't picky about their host as long as it has blood. They would be satisfied with a mouse or a moose, a cow or a crow. This is a problem for disease viruses that reproduce only in specific hosts.

After that first, satisfying, blood meal, the larval tick drops off the host, sheds its "skin" and transforms into the next life stage, a somewhat larger, eight-legged stage called a nymph. The nymph then goes a-questing once again, finds a new host, sucks up a second blood meal, drops to the ground once again, and molts into an adult. Adults quest, mate, suck blood (often these latter two at the same time), and this time when they drop off they soon die. Females lay eggs before they die though, starting the next generation.

As a confirmed tick-hater, it's somehow comforting to know that after I discard that jellybean size, blood-filled monstrosity that I plucked off myself or my dog, it will soon die even if I forget to squash it.

So here is a problem if you are a "bug" (virus or bacteria) hitching your evolutionary fate to being spread by ticks. Ticks only eat three meals in their lives and it takes at two meals for you to complete *your* life cycle, one meal to infect the tick, another for the tick to transmit you to a new host. Two out of only three possibilities doesn't seem like great transmission odds to me.

The other problem is with the way ticks suck. The business end of their mouths is basically a barbed hypodermic needle, which they insert into a blood vessel. That needle must do two things, suck blood and inject saliva. You thought ticks were gross just because they suck blood? What about that they also pump their saliva into you?

The saliva is necessary to keep the blood flowing. It contains a nice cocktail of local anesthetic, so you don't feel them, and other chemicals to keep the blood vessel open and the blood from coagulating. Disease organisms actually pass from the ticks to you in the saliva.

But with only a single needle ticks can't suck blood in one direction, and pump saliva in the other, at the same time. So they alternate. Pump saliva, suck blood, pump, suck, pump, and so on. This is why it takes days for a tick to fill itself on your blood. The deer tick, for instance, will spend 3-10 days gorging itself on your blood. And because disease-causing bacteria only move into the tick's saliva glands after they start feeding, it takes a day or more of feeding before the disease is likely to be transmitted.

By comparison, mosquitoes are models of elegance and efficiency.

First, let's put the blame—or credit—where it is due. All blood-sucking mosquitoes are females. Male mosquitoes, and mosquito larvae of both sexes, dine on other things.

The female mosquito's hypodermic sucking apparatus is different. It has two tubes, one for sucking blood, the other for pumping saliva. So they can multi-task, pumping saliva (and the Zika or Dengue virus) and sucking blood at the same time. So instead of taking days to fill up with blood like a tick, it takes them only a couple of minutes. Then they fly off to lay eggs before feeding again. It is only older females, who are on their second or later blood meal that transmit disease. They have to pick it up from an infected host on that first meal.

See what I mean? Elegant.

Don't get me wrong, ticks spread a list of diseases as long as your blood-filled arm—Lyme disease, Rocky Mountain Spotted Fever, tularemia, Ehrlichiosis, Powassan disease to name a few. Notice that you have heard of few of these. That's because most of them are rare.

Mosquitoes by contrast are such efficient disease spreaders that they are justifiably called the deadliest animal on the planet. They spread celebrity diseases—malaria, Dengue fever, yellow fever, West Nile virus, Rift Valley fever, Ross River fever, and a number of encephalitis-causing bugs. And now Zika. The World Health Organization calculates that more than a million people die each year thanks to mosquito transmitted diseases. That is efficiency.

You don't have to like them, but you do have to respect them.

VI.

Origins

DNA and the Story of our Species

W E will never know whether the dark-eyed, dark-skinned eight year old girl—we don't know her name, but let's call her Denise—was murdered, died of natural causes, or was simply interred in the Siberian cave where her remains were discovered.

Those remains consisted of only a pebble-size bone fragment from her pinkie finger. Yet thanks to the remarkable ability of modern scientists to extract and piece together the fragments of DNA trapped in that bone, her entire genome could be reconstructed. And her genome told us that Denise, who died some forty thousand years ago, belonged to a previously unknown human species.

Think about that. A new human species deduced from a fragment of a single forty thousand year old finger bone!

Aside from her genome, we know next to nothing about her species, now called Denisovans. Our sum of knowledge about them is that pinkie bone plus two teeth and a toe bone from other individuals. From her genes, we can guess pretty accurately her skin, eye, and hair color. But we have no idea what she, or Denisovans generally, looked like. Were they tall or short, stout or thin? Were their brains as big, or bigger, than ours? What sort of tools or weapons might they have used? Might they have made art? Had a language?

Although we know so little about Denisovans, we know a lot about another human species alive at the same time, Neanderthals. We've been finding Neanderthal artifacts, skulls, and skeletons since the mid-1800's. We know they lived in Europe and Asia for at least four hundred thousand years and vanished only about forty thousand years ago. They were bigger and stockier than we are. Surprisingly, they had a bigger brain too. Neanderthals probably also had a language, possibly many languages given how widespread they were. They used fire. They mourned and buried their dead. They painted figures on the walls of caves.

But until we managed to sequence Neanderthal DNA from some of the many skeletal remains in existence, we didn't realize that some of them also had red hair and light skin. We also never suspected that our own ancestors mated with them during that relatively brief period when we both occupied the same areas of Europe and Asia. As a consequence, today almost everyone not native to Africa has a couple of percent Neanderthal DNA.

For that matter, almost all non-African natives have a smidgeon of Denisovan DNA too. In fact, one Denisovan gene that helped them use oxygen particularly efficiently has been inherited by Himalayan sherpas and may be behind their ability to thrive at the high altitudes and ferry rich tourists to the top of Mount Everest for a living.

There was apparently considerable hanky-panky going on between these three human species—Denisovans, Neanderthals, and us—some tens of thousands of years ago.

For all it tells us about our relatively recent history, DNA plays little role in our knowledge of the earliest human history. DNA simply does not survive intact for millions of years. In warm, humid climates like tropical Africa where humans arose, it doesn't even last for tens of thousands of years. Preservation of ancient DNA like Denise's, requires the proper conditions, in her case a cool Siberian cave.

From abundant fossil evidence though, we know that humans arose in Africa, splitting off from our common ancestor with chimpanzees about six million years ago. In that sense, we are all Africans.

The DNA of living people confirms that African origin. Native Africans today have far more DNA diversity than the rest of the world combined, which is exactly what you would expect if people in the rest of the world descended from a small, adventurous group of Africans from one small corner of that continent. Recently researchers sequenced the DNA of hundreds of people from around the world discovering that although there may have been many migrations out of Africa, modern non-Africans virtually all descended from a wave of migrants about sixty thousand years ago. We also know that our DNA, that is, the DNA of the rest of the non-African world, is most closely related to modern Africans living in the northeast corner of Africa, where humans would have been able to walk out of Africa into present day Israel and the Arabian Peninsula when the sea level was a bit lower than it is today, and from there to the rest of the world.

In addition to these three human species living at the same time, there was also a fourth species—tiny humans, commonly called Flores man or "hobbits." Hobbits lived in isolation on some small islands in what today is Indonesia. No DNA from them, alas. The tropical climate is too warm and moist. We do have almost complete skeletal remains though.

Hobbits were three-and-a-half feet tall and weighed only about fifty pounds or so. That may seem surprising, but it isn't. It is well known to biologists that species that evolve on islands often become either much smaller or much larger than their mainland relatives depending on the island's ecology. Living with the hobbits, and probably being hunted by them, were pony-size elephants. Also, living with the hobbits, and possibly preying on them, were crocodile-size lizards that today we call Komodo dragons.

Three of the four human species alive during Denise's time—all except us—are now long gone. What happened to them?

Well, I don't want to point the finger too obviously at yours truly, but wherever and whenever our own species shows up, certain things seem to happen. Not long after we showed up in the Middle East, Neanderthals disappeared. Then we showed up in Europe and they vanished there too. Hobbits also disappeared about the same time that our species arrived on the Indonesian islands. The pony-size elephants disappeared around that time too. We don't yet know enough about the Denisovans to know if they vanished too soon after we arrived in Asia. I'm just saying, it looks suspicious. It may not be a smoking gun, but I wouldn't want to have to defend ourselves in front of a jury.

Nasty, Brutish, and Especially Short

THE English philosopher, Thomas Hobbs, writing in the seventeenth century, famously characterized human life as "nasty, brutish, and short." Since Hobbs' time, science has transformed our lives to an almost unimaginable extent. To appreciate how lucky we are to be living today, it is worth recalling what life and health were like in a pre-scientific world. Hobbs may have understated how miserable things were.

Consider the exceptionally well-documented life of one prominent Englishman living in Hobbs' time, Samuel Pepys, who is remembered today for the diary he kept during the tumultuous 1660's when London was ravaged by plague, fire, and war. At that time, life was indeed short. Life expectancy was twenty-something. Diseases struck seemingly out of nowhere, killing this person, sparing that one, for no obvious reason. When you began feeling feverish and ill, as happened often, you or your physician had no idea if you would be fine in a few days or dead in a week. The brutality of such an existence is evident in the Pepys family. He was the fifth of eleven children. By the time he was eight, all four of his older siblings had died. Two of his younger brothers survived into their thirties and a one sister made it to age forty-nine. Everyone else died in infancy or adolescence. It wasn't impossible to live a reasonably long life—Pepys himself lived to age seventy—it was just unlikely.

Because of the mysterious randomness of death, life had a special urgency. So Pepys married as soon as he decided he was prosperous enough to start a family at age twenty-two. His bride, Elizabeth, was fourteen, not an uncommon age to wed at the time. Later, despairing that his younger sister, Paulina, would ever marry, Pepys wrote in his diary "she grows old and must be disposed of one way or another." Paulina was twenty-three.

Hygiene was an unknown concept. Sewage was dumped into the streets. Water was drunk from the rivers into which the sewage drained. People seldom bathed or washed clothes. Living quarters were shared with rats, cats, mice, lice, fleas and bedbugs. During the great plague that swept through London in 1665 killing one-fifth of its inhabitants, Pepys may have been protected because having slept in flea- infested beds his whole life, he noted in his diary that fleas seemed to like other people much more than they liked him. He was lucky. Fleas were of course responsible for transmitting the plague from rats to humans.

Medical treatment, if you had the misfortune to require it, was a mixture of brutality, ignorance, and superstition. A popular treatment for just about any ailment was "bleeding," the practice of draining a certain amount of blood from the body. Except in extraordinary circumstances, bleeding has no known medical benefit, and if done to excess can be dangerous. George Washington was bled so enthusiastically and repeatedly during his final illness, that many modern physicians think it was the bleeding, not the infection, that killed him. Pepys had himself bled several times per year as a disease prevention measure.

During his wife's fatal illness (she died of a fever probably due to contaminated food or water at age twenty-nine), her physicians treated her more gently, if not more effectively. That treatment consisted of shaving her head and placing pigeons around her feet. Those remedies had been tried on the Queen a few years earlier and she had recovered, so why not?

Pain was ubiquitous and you had no choice but to live with it. Pepys' wife suffered from repeated toothaches. He was tortured by a bladder stone from the time he was a boy until age twenty-five when no longer able to endure the pain, he had it surgically removed. That surgery was performed while he was strapped to a table and held down by strong men. His incision never completely healed and probably contributed to his death when it burst open again forty-five years later. Still, he was lucky. Surgery of any type killed more people than it saved because of the infections that inevitably followed in a pre-antiseptic era.

So thank your lucky stars you are alive today and consider that the difference between today and Pepys' time is due to the development of science. So thank science too.

Fire, Fire Burning Bright

A H, the rites of summer. Picnics in the park, crowds at the beaches and public swimming pools, raging wildfires out west.

Why is the western U.S. so prone to wildfires? For once, we can't entirely blame people. Despite what Smokey the Bear might say, wildfires have never required human carelessness. In fact, we know from the evidence of fossilized charcoal that wildfires were a normal part of nature for hundreds of millions of years before humans existed.

The master fire starter has always been lightning. There are about a hundred lightning strikes per second—that's right, *per second*—somewhere on earth, so wildfires start all the time. What happens after lightning ignites them—the scope and scale of the resulting fire—will depend on the weather and the amount and type of combustible fuel.

The West is not so prone to wildfires because of the amount of rain it gets, so much as because of the *timing* of the rain it gets. Unlike most of the east, almost all parts of the West have a pronounced dry season during the summer months. Even nominally wet places like Portland and Seattle get little summer rain, less than 10 percent of the year's total. In the East on the other hand, summer months typically get as much rain as any other months. These prolonged, dry western summers parch the vegetation making it particularly combustible when isolated lightning storms appear. Interestingly, the worst wildfire seasons will often follow particularly rainy ones, because more rain in the spring and fall means more abundant vegetation. That vegetation turns into wildfire fuel once it dries out.

Also, the West has deserts, sources of hot, dry winds. In fact, the most ferocious winds out west are those that blow in off the desert. Hot dry winds are ideal for fanning small wildfires into massive, fast-moving infernos. Southern California's Santa Ana winds, howling in from the Mojave, routinely reach hurricane force. In the East, our big winds and thunderstorms usually accompany heavy rain. Soggy vegetation burns poorly.

Humans do come into the picture when we think about our habit of working heroically to suppress wildfires. This, of course, allows the accumulation of unprecedented amounts of dry underbrush wherever it hadn't burned recently.

We started seriously suppressing forest fires after what was known as the Great Fire of 1910, which burned an area of Idaho and Montana the size of Maryland and killed eight-six people. The Forest Service subsequently built thousands of fire lookout towers in remote areas and hired "smokejumpers" to parachute into these areas to combat fires. At one point, Forest Service policy even declared—without apparent irony—that all wildfires, no matter how remote, were to be suppressed by 10 a.m. the morning after they were spotted. During World War II, protecting our forests was deemed a matter of national security. Smokey the Bear was concocted to publicize the fight against wildfires.

By the 1960's the Forest Service realized that this manic fire suppression policy was a mistake. It was even admitted that setting controlled burns at appropriate times and places could actually help prevent catastrophic fires. How important are previous burns in helping control wildfires? Remember that enormous "Thomas" wildfire of 2017—one of the biggest ones in modern California history, scorching more than 280 thousand acres? It was only finally controlled when it contacted areas where previous fires had burned off most of the ground fuel.

Finally—you knew it was coming—climate change has increased temperatures and prolonged droughts and dry seasons in a number of parts of the world and will continue to do so. As I write in September 2021, the top eight largest California wildfires have occurred since 2017 and fire season isn't over. California and the rest of the western United States isn't the only place burning regularly on an apocalyptic scale. In recent years forest fires raged out of control every summer in much of Europe, and Australia has suffered more than one apocalyptic fire in recent years.

These days wildfires are notorious for the destruction they cause. Ironically, for most of human history, wildfire was our friend. After all, before we lived in permanent settlements and became farmers, we had no structures that they could destroy. Before we knew how to start fires ourselves, we could capture and preserve flames from wildfires in campfires, torches, and as embers. Fire was invaluable to ancient humans, who could use it to scare off predators, keep warm, and cook food. With cooking, many foods become softer, tastier, and easier to digest. Previously inedible roots and shoots were made edible, even tasty, with cooking. Harvard anthropologist Richard Wrangham thinks that our early discovery of cooking is a big reason for our evolutionary success relative to other primates.

For millennia humans also managed their landscapes with fire. Early European settlers to the Americas noticed how park-like the landscape was. Widely-spaced trees were spread throughout grasslands—grasslands that were maintained by fires purposely started by native Americans. These grasslands attracted deer, elk, and bison making hunting easier. Australian aborigines carried "fire sticks" wherever they went to start small scale fires to clear underbrush for similar purposes. So did a number of the indigenous people of Africa and South America.

Wildfires have occurred regularly enough in areas with the right climate that it has profoundly shaped some ecosystems. Grassland ecosystems like the prairies of North America were largely maintained by fire before they were plowed into farmland. Southern California chaparral is another one of those fire-dependent ecosystems as are many western forests.

So is the longleaf pine ecosystem, formerly covering some ninety million acres along the coastal plains of the southeastern U.S. from Virginia down to Florida and around to eastern Texas. Native Americans played a large role the regular burning this ecosystem requires. Now reduced to less than 5 percent of its former area thanks to excessive logging and fire suppression, longleaf pine barrens are distinguished by their open park-like look as well as some of the highest biological diversity outside the tropics. The beauty and worth of this ecosystem is finally being appreciated and efforts to restore it, including the use of controlled burns, is ongoing.

So historically sometimes wildfires have been our friend, sometimes our enemy. Put another way, the fire giveth, and it taketh away.

The Beast that Built Civilization

A LTHOUGH the last one died in western Poland in 1627, you can make a good case that the animal species most responsible for who we humans are today was the aurochs. That's aurochs singular—ochs as in ox.

It was an enormous beast, looking something like a modern Spanish fighting bull only three times bigger. If its representation in Ice Age cave art is any indication, humans had enormous respect for the aurochs. It was fast, fierce, and fearless. Aurochsen were a source of meat and a source of danger. Eventually they were a source of civilization as I'll explain. We thanked them by hunting them to extinction.

The aurochs was the wild ancestor of the modern cow, bull, steer, heifer, ox—many names for one species.

For millennia the aurochs had turned grass into meat for us hunters. It turned grass into hide as well, providing us with clothing, shelter, straps, belts, cords, and thongs. Its bones could be honed into daggers, its horns fashioned into drinking vessels. Its fat provided oil for lamps, so we could see at night or meander inside dark caves to paint its picture. Once domesticated, roughly ten thousand years ago, and trained to drag a crude plow through hard packed earth, the aurochs opened up large tracts of land—vastly more land than a man with a digging stick could till—to agriculture. It provided nourishment for these fields in the form of manure. There was virtually no part of it that went to waste.

Our new large agricultural fields and the meat from our—let's now call them—cattle allowed us to stop hunting and gathering and settle down. We could produce all the food we needed locally. Once feeding ourselves became a part-time job, we had the leisure to develop writing, mathematics, architecture, become craftsmen and merchants. Those bovine descendants of the aurochs helped us invent civilization.

For those of us whose ancestors were long-time cattle herders, it also provided us a nutritious new adult beverage, milk. There are five thousand species of mammals on earth. All nourish their young with milk. Only one species, humans, continues to drink milk as adults.

The main carbohydrate in milk is lactose. To digest lactose requires an enzyme called lactase, which infants of all mammals produce. However, once the infants are weaned, the lactase-producing gene is turned off. Drinking milk after your lactase gene is turned off is no fun. Instead of a fine, nutritious, thirst-quenching drink, it wreaks havoc on your intestines, giving you diarrhea, bloating, gas, abdominal pain, the very opposite of fun.

Like all other mammals, most of the world's current population cannot drink milk as adults. Only about one-third of us, the one-third whose ancestors raised cattle for millennia, can. This includes most northern Europeans and traditional cattle-herding people in Africa and the Middle East. Mutations in our genome about six thousand years ago broke the "off" switch for our lactase gene. Lactase was turned on for life. You can understand the advantage. During times of drought or famine, cow's milk or the milk from other species we had domesticated by then, namely goats and sheep, could provide an additional source of food and drink. Those without the lactose-tolerance mutations would be less likely to survive through these hard times.

Once we figured out that milk and milk products like cheese, butter, and yogurt could be a part of our normal adult diet, it opened up the important possibility, many millennia later, for French cuisine.

The lucky lactose-tolerant people of the world began selectively breeding certain cattle for faster growth to give us abundant beef. Other cattle were selectively bred for greater and greater milk production. A dairy cow today produces about twenty-three thousand pounds of milk per year, at least five times as much as required to feed its one calf. Modern cow milk is nutritionally quite a bit like human breast milk. It has about the same amount of fat and lactose as human milk, which means that we have been genetically programmed to like its taste, at least when we are young.

Today cow's milk represents about 90 percent of the world's milk consumption. However, some people drink goat's milk which is lower in fat but higher in protein than cow's milk. Milk from horses, moose, sheep, camels, yak, and reindeer is popular in some places. We might be able to do better though. Polar bear milk has almost ten times as much fat and protein as cow's milk, almost no lactose. It's the consistency of runny butter. It would be a power drink for the lactose-intolerant—and they would need the all the power they could get—if they wanted to try milking polar bears.

In one sense, we may have finally returned the favor that the aurochs granted us ten thousand years ago. We have populated the world their descendants. There probably never were more than a million or so aurochses on earth at any one time. But there are now one and a half *billion* cows on earth. Whether that is compensation enough for having given us civilization and French cuisine, you be the judge.

Mummy Dearest

O NE of the few traits that distinguish humans from any other species is our obsession with preserved corpses. Sometimes nature cooperates with this obsession. For instance, in dry climates such as Egypt, Peru, and western China mummifying human remains occurs easily and naturally. Also, the peat bogs of northern Europe, because their soil is so depleted of oxygen, have provided us with nearly two thousand exquisitely-preserved corpses from as long as ten thousand years ago.

Of course, people will always improve upon nature if they can. So we've managed to find our own ways of preserving the flesh of our dearly departed even where the climate doesn't cooperate. Many of the techniques for doing so are summarized in the title of a fiendishly funny children's book, *Mummies: Dried, Tanned, Sealed, Drained, Frozen, Embalmed, Stuffed, Wrapped, and Smoked...and We're Dead Serious* (National Geographic Press, 2010).

There are few things in life better than being able to pursue your childhood fascinations with yucky (to use the scientific term) things under the cover of a dead (couldn't help it) serious adult purpose. Throw in some detective work and you can see how the study of mummies using modern science can be so appealing but also so informative. For instance, the six-and-a-half foot tall heavily bearded, light-haired mummified man buried three millennia ago in the western China desert revealed that culture began migrating between Europe and eastern Asia much earlier than anyone had previously supposed.

Mummies can also teach us many things about the daily lives and deaths of people living in remote historical periods and places—what they ate, what diseases they had, how old they were when they died, and sometimes what killed them. Oetzi, for instance, is a five thousand year old, particularly well-studied European ice mummy. We know more about Oetzi than probably any other ancient mummy, from the contents of his last meal (deer meat and herb bread) to how many times he had been sick in the six months before he died (three), and even thanks to analysis of his DNA, that he was lactose intolerant and at high risk for cardiovascular disease had he lived long enough. He died at about age forty-five, which is a reasonably long life for five thousand years ago. We also know from DNA in the blood stains on his knife and on an arrow that he carried that Oetzi not long before he died had killed as many as three people. In an instance of ancient justice, he himself was killed by an arrow in the back, probably as he fled from one or more attackers. Life was clearly no stroll in the park in Copper Age Europe.

In recent years, scientists on a world mummy tour have been using X-ray CT scanners, which give nice three dimensional images of the inside of the body, to discover that atherosclerosis, the thickening of artery walls that predisposes us to heart attacks and strokes as we age, was common in people from virtually every part of the ancient world living virtually every life style. How could they tell this? They detected calcium deposits, similar to the hard white scale left in pipes and teapots by hard water, in mummies' artery walls. Calcification like this is a hallmark of atherosclerosis.

This doesn't mean that these mummies died of heart attacks though. Very few, if any, probably did. They died too young, average age of only thirty-six years. You can live a long time without any symptoms with calcified arteries. What the mummies do tell us is that atherosclerosis has been a central feature of human biology for a very long time. It is not a modern aberration of fast food and couch potato-dom. It starts early in life, as early as your twenties, and gets progressively worse with time and bad lifestyle choices. Every species has its own particular vulnerabilities to aging. This one is apparently ours.

The other thing the mummy study highlights is how successful modern medical science has been at combatting this particular vulnerability. The twentieth century exposed our vulnerability to atherosclerosis as we began living long enough to commonly die of heart attacks. In 1910 when heart disease first passed tuberculosis and influenza to become America's number one killer, only about 10 percent of us died from heart diseases because life expectancy was still only forty-eight years. By 1960 when life expectancy hit seventy years for the first time, heart diseases killed nearly 40 percent of Americans. In recent years though, heart disease deaths have plummeted. Thanks to less smoking, more low-fat food options, better medical surveillance and treatment, as well as blood pressure and cholesterol lowering medications, heart diseases now kill fewer than a quarter of us. They kill us at later ages than ever before as well. In fact, after a hundred year reign as our number one killer, for decades killing more than twice as many people as any other cause, heart disease may soon slip to number two (behind cancer) in the cause-of-death ranking.

The biology of mummies is no longer our destiny.

VII.

Aging Gracefully

How Long Can Humans Live?

ONE year before General George Custer was killed in the Battle of the Little Bighorn and the same year that two American colleges for the first time played one another in a game that we would recognize today as American football, a baby girl was born in the small town of Arles in southern France, who would go on to achieve something no human has come close to before or since. Her name was Jeanne Calment.

She was a small woman, not quite reaching five feet in height. When she was thirteen, she met a man who later would become famous, the artist Vincent van Gogh. She remembered him as "'very ugly, ungracious, impolite." At the age of twenty-one she married Fernand Calment, who shared her last name because their paternal grandfathers were brothers. Eighteen months later, her first and only child, Yvonne, was born. Yvonne died of pneumonia at age thirty-six, leaving behind Frederic, her eight year-old son to be raised by Jeanne and Fernand, his grandparents. Frederic tragically died in a car crash, like his mother at age thirty-six. So the remarkable Jeanne Calment left no direct descendants.

When Madame Calment was born, French women could expect to live less than forty-nine years. The feat that she achieved—that no one else has approached—was that she lived 122 years, 164 days or until the presidency of Bill Clinton—from Custer to Clinton, as I think of it . That is more than three years longer than any other known person. She held what I have called the world's most dangerous job—being the oldest person alive—for more than nine years.

I have been thinking of Jeanne Calment recently, because of an analysis of the world's oldest people in the journal *Science*, arguably our most prestigious scientific journal. That analysis has been wildly misinterpreted by much of the world's press, so I thought I might clarify its meaning.

The analysis claims that a person's yearly risk of dying no longer increases with age after age 105. The researchers reached this conclusion by looking at death rates of almost four thousand Italians—nearly 90 percent of them women—who had lived 105 years or longer. That claim has been interpreted as good news for those who want to live as long or longer than Jeanne Calment and to mean, incredibly, that there is no limit to how long humans can live.

Sorry folks, if you aspire to break Mme. Calment's record, I'm all for you keeping up the effort, but don't get your hopes up despite this report. Here's why.

It is well-known that the risk of dying indeed climbs steadily throughout adult life. It doubles, in fact, about every eight years, which is why your life insurance rates double at about the same rate. Insurance companies make money by knowing these things. Doing a little arithmetic, you can see that whatever your chance of dying at, say, age forty, it is twice that by age forty-eight, four times that by age fifty-four, and sixty-five times that by age 105, which according to this new report is when the death rate stops increasing.

Today, of course, many more people live to 105 years of age than at any time in the three hundred thousand year history of our species. Still, it is rare enough to make you a minor celebrity.

So let's imagine that you've eaten a healthy diet, done your regular exercise, not smoked, drunk alcohol moderately, and maybe most importantly chosen long-lived parents. You have become widely celebrated in your community for reaching your 105th birthday and your annual chance of living another year remains steady from now on.

That's great, but don't bank on living a great deal longer. According to the new report's own data, your chance of surviving each year is now a steady fifty-three percent. If true, that means you only have a one in twenty-five chance of reaching your 110th birthday, not bad but also not likely. You have less than one chance in six hundred of reaching the ripe old age of 115 and your chances of reaching Jeanne Calment's age? Less than one in fifty-seven thousand. True, these odds are not zero, but if they make you particularly optimistic about living that long, I advise you to never enter a casino.

A reporter recently asked me whether this new research had made me more optimistic about winning the wager I have with demographer, Jay Olshansky. That "billion dollar" wager made in 2001 is whether the first person to reach 150 years of age is already alive. I still say "yes" and I still expect to win. But not because we've discovered that death rates have stopped increasing at age 105. In fact, by my calculations of this steady reported survival rate, it would take almost *four trillion (!)* people reaching age 105 for me to have an even chance of winning my bet. That is more than five hundred times the total number of people currently on earth, folks.

I don't know about you, but I would call that a limit.

So, no, I do not expect to win my wager because death rates stop increasing at age 105. I do expect to win because we are discovering therapies that actually slow the rate of aging. Several of these medications are about to start human trials. If successful, they will slow down that eight year doubling time of our probability of dying.

Medical advances that change our aging rate is why I feel destined to win my wager. Of course, this means Jeanne Calment's longevity record, like records of virtually any sort, will finally be broken too.

The Dick Clark Effect

ICK Clark, for more thirty years host of the teenager television dance show *American Bandstand*, died in 2012 at age eighty-two. For those of you who don't remember him, Dick Clark was famous for never aging. That is, for decades his appearance never seemed to change. When I was a teenager, he looked like an old man of twenty-three or so. When I was in my forties, he looked like a whippersnapper of twenty-three or so. So far as I can tell from the photos published with his obituary he may have still looked twenty-three or so to the very end. An interesting question that people like Dick Clark make you ponder is whether looking young means you're staying young physically. Call it the Dick Clark effect, not to be confused with the Joan Rivers effect, in which surgical attempts to look younger simply make you look ghoulish instead.

Danish scientist Kaare Christensen ingeniously tested the Dick Clark effect using simple passport style photographs of nearly five hundred pairs of same sex twins seventy years old or older. About half were identical twins, about half non-identical. Without telling them they would be looking at twins, he then asked a group of nurses to look at all the photos and guess the age of each person. On one day they looked at all the photos of one twin of each set, on another day the other set. Several years later, when a significant number of the twins had died, he found surprising support for the Dick Clark effect. Averaging all the nurses' age guesses, the twin who looked older turned out to be more likely to die first. When the average nurses' age guesses for twins differed by at least two years, the older looking twin died first three-quarters of the time. In fact, looking a year older was more hazardous to one's health than *actually being* a year older!

Christensen thought that because of the nurses' experience with sick people they might be especially good at picking up subtle signs of ill health, so he repeated the experiment with a group of lay people doing the age estimates. Astonishingly, they did just as well as the nurses at predicting which twin would die first.

Understanding why some people look young (or old) for their age is complicated. It involves genetics, of course. At what age will you lose your hair or gain significant weight or develop facial wrinkles? For the identical twins, though, genetics shouldn't be an issue. They are after all genetically identical. Yet the older looking identical twin died first 60 percent of the time. It also involves lifestyle. Did one twin drink alcohol more than the other? Did one exercise more? Eat more veggies? For whatever reason, we humans seem to be pretty good at assessing relative health from nothing more than a passport-style photograph. It would be intriguing to see how much (if any) better we might do if instead of only seeing a photograph we could also hold a brief conversation with each one or watch them walk across a room. I personally would like to know whether trained medical professionals could do better at this than lay people. I would like to think so, but wouldn't bet the farm on it.

Getting back to Dick Clark. An average American man dies at about age seventy-nine these days, so Dick Clark living to age eight-two did seem—at least in a small way—to embody the Dick Clark effect.

Baby, It's Cold in Here

"**I** PLAN to live forever because I'm having my head frozen."

You never know who might be sitting next to you on an airplane. This fellow looked normal enough—for a Californian. Why would he whisper such a confession into the ear of a perfect stranger? Maybe he had peeked at something I was typing on my laptop and saw some words like "longevity" or "aging"? The funny thing is that I knew exactly what he was talking about.

Cryonics is the idea—or more precisely, the hope—that by freezing your body after death, preserving it for decades or even centuries, future scientists will be able to cure whatever ailed you and bring your body back to life. Why future scientists would want to do this isn't exactly clear. Maybe there will be no more pressing problems in the future than bringing dead people back to life. Anyway, assuming they wanted to for some reason, the real hope is not that only your body would be brought back to life, but that in doing so *you* would be brought back to life, something like awakening after surgery.

Cryonics embodies a rather touching faith in scientific progress. Or maybe it embodies only an exceptional fear of death. In either case, it raises some interesting philosophical questions. What would it take for that newly re-animated body to still be "you"? With a little tweaking of existing technology, we could create a genetically identical copy of you as we've already done in mice, dogs, and a number of other species, by cloning a cell from your current body. But that wouldn't really be you, because it wouldn't have your memories or experiences.

Memories are the key. Thus, the frozen head. As long as your brain still contains your memories, your reanimated head could be thought of as you. As for the rest of your body, any science sophisticated enough to bring your head back to life should no doubt be able to give you any body you wanted instead of a just replica of your previous body. I'll have to think about whose body I'd like.

Besides keeping only your head saves money. Cryonics is not cheap. Prices I've seen range from about thirty thousand dollars for a budget deal to several hundred thousand, not including the currently unknown cost of re-animating you and attaching a body to that head. To preserve your body requires ultra-cold freezing with liquid nitrogen. Long lines of freezers packed with bodies like so many popsicles uses a lot of that expensive liquid nitrogen and takes up a lot of space, for who knows how many years? Freezers full of hat box-size containers are comparatively economical, can be packed efficiently, and so are good for the profit margin.

There do seem to be some formidable scientific barriers though, even if you assume that re-growing a body on your revivified head is feasible. For one thing, no one has brought something as simple as even a single cell back from death, not that I'm sure how much effort has been put into doing so. Another issue is that our memories are thought to be a product of the number and strength of very delicate electrical connections among our billions of brain cells. Memory can be seriously disrupted by something as simple as a bang on the head. So preserving those things through a complete cessation of all brain electrical activity and the inevitable postmortem damage to brain cells seems more than a little far-fetched. Also, if you died of a stroke or dementia, sorry you're out of luck. Those critical memory centers were destroyed even before you died.

Whatever your opinion of cryonics, to my mind the head thing itself needs some rethinking. The important thing obviously is preservation of the brain. So why not freeze just the brain rather than the whole head? If science proceeds to the point where they can re-grow a complete body, surely it will be able to give me a better head to house my brain. Why would I want to look like I looked when I died, if I could look like, say, a young Brad Pitt instead? Let's see. Brad Pitt's head, maybe LeBron James' body. Do I want to be a movie star or an athletic hero in my next life? Perhaps both? Okay, where do I sign up?

Hormones and Health

T age seventy-two, French-American Doctor Charles-Édouard Brown-Séquard could feel his energy flagging. He felt his mental powers waning and couldn't get a good night's sleep anymore. And so the good doctor did what any of us might have done. He whipped up a cocktail of macerated dog and guinea pig testicles and injected himself with it. Thus was born the idea that topping up your dwindling hormones as you age is a key to prolonging health and vigor.

Presenting the results of this experiment on himself at a scientific conference a few months later, Brown-Séquard reported that he felt ten years younger, stronger, more energetic, mentally sharper. Now he slept like a baby. Even though the year was 1889, today we would say that news of this elixir went viral. Within six months American doctors, not about to pass up an obvious commercial opportunity, had administered the Brown-Séquard (let's just call it B-S for short) elixir to more than twelve thousand desperate men, including one thirty-two year-old Hall of Fame baseball pitcher, Jim "Pud" Galvin, who was trying to hang on to a fading athletic career. Some things don't change.

Today, we have the commercial descendants of Brown-Séquard still hawking hope and hormones. Is there any evidence that they work?

It depends on what you mean by "work." A good case, by far the best case, for giving extra hormones to otherwise healthy people is the replacement of female reproductive hormones that drop rather abruptly during and after menopause.

Until the twenty-first century, in fact, the evidence for the health benefits of replacing female hormones after menopause seemed quite compelling. Observational studies—those in which researchers compare one group of people taking some treatment such as hormone replacement with a similar group not getting the treatment and then monitor how the two groups' health progresses over time—looked promising. This sort of evidence, though common in human studies is relatively weak, because it is difficult to be sure that your two groups are similar in all the relevant ways. Still, the observational studies up until the twenty-first century presented a pretty compelling case that hormone replacement in women after menopause, besides reducing common problems like sudden hot flashes and night sweats, also protected against heart attacks, strokes, osteoporosis, perhaps even Alzheimer's disease. In my 1997 book on aging, I even somewhat embarrassingly wrote "…if [estrogen] came from plants or had an exotic name, any drug with this sort of clinical record would be heralded as a miracle drug for slowing the aging process."

This conclusion was based purely on observational studies, some women chose to take hormone replacement, others didn't. But much stronger evidence comes from experiments in which you randomly assign people to either get the hormones or a dummy treatment called a placebo, then compare health in the two groups as time passes. These experiments are called clinical trials or sometimes just "trials" in the popular press. The dummy treatment is important—one of the most important parts of any human experiment—because it is well known that when people think they are getting a treatment that will make them better, they actually do get better, at least temporarily. Interestingly, placebos are even more effective when people receiving them are deceived into thinking they are getting expensive drugs rather than inexpensive ones.

The first large experimental trial of post-menopausal hormone replacement, called the Women's Health Initiative, exploded the conventional medical wisdom of its broad health-promoting, life-prolonging effects. In fact, that study was stopped early because women in the hormone replacement group were having too many health problems. Heart disease went up, not down. Strokes went up, not down. Hip fractures were reduced though.

Layers of complexity are buried in this study. For instance, results varied depending on the women's age and whether they had previously had their ovaries removed (which affected the hormone cocktail they received). So whether hormone replacement should be considered for any individual woman is a decision that should be reached in consultation with her physician. However, the evidence is clear that hormone replacement in post-menopausal women is not the elixir of youth that many of us had hoped.

What about men? You can hardly watch a football game or read a sports magazine without seeing advertisements suggesting that maybe your T (=testosterone) is low, particularly if your performance *down there* doesn't seem to be what it used to be. And then there are those men whose faces look like your grandfather but whose bodies look like Olympic athletes that you see in virtually any glossy airplane magazine. All they needed to transform the body shape of a tomato to that of an apple was a little pep up with human growth hormone or hGH as it is abbreviated, right? Both T and hGH will in fact build muscle and reduce fat, particularly when combined with an exercise program. This is why anabolic steroids (synthetic versions of testosterone) and hGH are favored by aging athletes looking for an edge. There is no equivalent of the Women's Health Initiative to test the health impact of these drugs though.

Two observations suggest that caution might be in order before starting your hormone treatment fellows. First, we know for certain that the best way to kill a laboratory mouse early is to overload it with growth hormone and the best way to make it live longer is to eliminate its growth hormone. This has been shown many times in rigorous experiments. Maybe humans are different. Who knows? Second, two admittedly weak but provocative studies have compared longevity in normal men with those who had been castrated—men, in other words, who had had their T reduced to virtually zero. In one study the castrated men lived thirteen years longer than the normal men. In the other study, the castrated men lived twenty years longer. Let me emphasize that these were uncontrolled, observational studies, so men, don't try this at home. The evidence that castration is life- and health-giving is provocative as I say, but not close to conclusive. It might give you second thoughts, however, about supplementing your natural hormones.

What about our friends, Dr. Brown-Séquard and Pud Galvin? The good doctor lived four more years after discovering his elixir, not exactly a testimonial for it but not bad for a seventy something man in the late 1800's. Pud Galvin, on the other hand, temporarily found new baseball life. In the finest baseball tradition, he didn't inject the testicle elixir. He drank it. The effects, thanks to Dr. Placebo, were immediate. The next day he pitched a shutout, and even though he was a typically weak-hitting pitcher, got two hits. The rest of his life and career weren't so successful though. He had won an amazing 337 games over a fourteen year career before starting on the

B-S elixir, becoming in fact the first three hundred game winner in base-ball history. However, he won only another thirty-seven games before he retired three years later at age thirty-five. Pud died prematurely at age forty-five. Alas, history is silent on whether he continued the elixir in retirement.

John Brinkley, a Colorful Old Goat

ONE thing about colorful scoundrels is that with the passage of time, we tend to remember how colorful they were and forget about their scoundrel side. Case in point: John Romulus Brinkley, *Doctor* Brinkley after he purchased a shady medical degree. Whatever inspired him to suggest to forty-six year old farmer Bill Stittsworth that what he needed to cure the pains of aging was a spanking new pair of goat testicles, we may never know. That's right, goat testicles. Later he also surgically implanted goat ovaries into Mrs. Stittsworth and when they had a (human) baby not long afterwards, Doc Brinkley's fortune was made. Goat "glands," as they were euphemistically called, did not just rejuvenate that part of the body you might expect, Brinkley later reported they also erased wrinkles, returned gray hair to black, cured mental retardation, criminality, and dozens of other ailments.

The story of John Brinkley, the high Priest of bogus hormone replacement, is told with masterful verve and wit by Pope Brock in his 2008 book *Charlatan.* Brinkley became famous in tiny Milford, Kansas, where he met the Stittsworths and made pseudo-medical history. With little training and no talent for surgery, even when he operated sober, he killed at least a few dozen previously healthy people in his hospital and no one knows how many more were maimed or died later at home. Despite the rising carnage, he knew how to keep Milford's city fathers happy, using his increasing wealth to build a new sewer system, sidewalks, a post office, and even new uniforms for the town's Little League team, the Brinkley Goats.

If not a skilled surgeon, Brinkley was a marketing genius. Among the first to realize the potential of radio as a promotional medium, he built

his own radio station, launching into the night sky his soothing and se-
ductive con man's voice. His on-air soliloquys were masterworks of im-
provisation—combinations of religious homilies, cornpone nostalgia, and
of course medical advice on the virtues of testicle implants. The healing
powers of his personally-designed medicines, available only at his chain of
affiliated pharmacies, cured pretty much anything that goat glands didn't.
He couldn't talk all day and all night, so he filled out his airtime with entertainment. With his grifter's instinct for what an audience wanted to hear,
by 1930 his radio station, KFKB, had become the most popular station in
the country. That was the same year his depredations on a gullible public
became too much even in Kansas; the state Medical Board revoked his
medical license and the federal government pulled his radio license. So he
did what scoundrels often do. He moved to Texas.

Del Rio, Texas, nestled on the Rio Grande, had been recruiting Doc
Brinkley for some time. The money he pulled in—by this time he was richer
than chocolate cheesecake—and his civic good deeds, looked like just what
a poor border town crippled by the Depression needed. Brinkley exploited
the less-regulated radio industry on the Mexican side of the border. Instead of the puny five thousand watt station he was limited to in Kansas,
his Mexican station, XER, eventually powered up to a million watts and
could be heard in every state and at least fifteen foreign countries. Rumor
had it that in Del Rio, you could pick up XER on your dental fillings. With
a national audience, XER's entertainers exploded into a veritable galaxy of
country music stars from Patsy Montana and Gene Autry to Jimmie Rodg-
ers and the Carter family.

Ultimately, an ill-advised lawsuit brought him down. Morris Fishbein,
a real doctor and editor of the *Journal of the American Medical Associa-
tion*, called Brinkley a medical charlatan in print. Brinkley, incensed, sued
him for libel. The trial lasted only a few days with the jury finding that
Brinkley "should be considered a charlatan and a quack in the ordinary,
well-understood meaning of those words." The trial transcripts make for
some amusing reading, such as when Brinkley tries to explain to the jury
how his overpriced injections of colored tap water could boost the immune
system. The trial outcome unleashed a flurry of other lawsuits against him
and the IRS launched an investigation of his taxes. Somewhat later, the US
Postal service began investigating him for mail fraud.

Brinkley declared bankruptcy in San Antonio in 1941 and died at age
fifty-six less than a year later. His mansion in Del Rio is still the fanciest

estate in town and has been designated a Texas historic landmark. The plaque in front of his mansion today describes Dr. Brinkley as "promoting controversial medical practices." You might similarly argue that John Dillinger promoted controversial business practices. Dillinger killed fewer people though.

Brinkley's pseudo-medical heirs are still with us. "Anti-aging" pills, potions, lotions, and injections still bring in truckloads of money and still have much the same rejuvenation properties as goat testicles.

The Top Ten Old Stars

O N her twenty-fifth birthday, my daughter Molly announced to me that she "felt so old." She got little sympathy from her father about her tragic predicament, but she did make me take note that the age we think of as "old" is all relative.

If you are a female competitive gymnast, for instance, you are old—that is, past your athletic prime—by the time you reach your twenties. The average age of the women's all-around gymnastics champion in the last four Olympics was less than eighteen years. Chinese gymnast Dong Fangxiao won medals at the World Championships when she was thirteen years old, too young to even compete legally (as a consequence she was later stripped of her titles).

Baseball and basketball players reach peak performance in their late twenties and grow old and typically retire in their thirties. Time is more forgiving to scientists and artists, who can remain at peak productivity into their sixties or even beyond. Historian Jacques Barzun, for instance, published his biggest and best book, *Dawn to Decadence*, at the age of ninety-three.

But certain people seem to defy time regardless of their field. They perform at levels we simply can't believe for someone of their calendar age. Often they do it because of exceptionally hard work, but sometimes it's mostly luck (inheriting the right genes). In any case, it seems to me that we ought to have awards for these exceptional performers, if for nothing else than as an inspiration to the rest of us. Let's call these people "Old Stars" rather than "All Stars." As someone who studies aging for a living, I present my personal top ten list of Old Stars.

At number ten, Jeanne Calment makes the list for simply drawing breath longer than anyone else, 122 years, 164 days. During her more than nine year reign as the world's oldest living person, she became famous for being old, as she would be the first to tell you. She had quite the mischievous wit, which may have helped her cope. My favorite quote. "Even at my age I've only got one wrinkle. And I'm sitting on it."

At number nine, we have Dave Taylor, who at age thirty-eight fractured his spine and pelvis and suffered horrific burns when a movie stunt went horribly wrong, as he leapt off a forty foot high burning building during the filming of the aptly named movie *Death Wish*. To prove he still had what it takes, he publicly repeated the stunt, without broken bones this time, at the age of sixty-four for the benefit of his favorite charity.

Number eight is Nolan Ryan, legendary baseball pitcher, threw his seventh no-hit game for the Texas Rangers, striking out sixteen batters, at the age of forty-four, the same age as his pitching coach.

At number seven, Nolan Ryan again. The legendary baseball pitcher and barnyard tough Texan, still pitching at age forty-six, pummeled the tar out of twenty-six year old Robin Ventura, who made the mistake of charging the pitching mound after being plunked on the shoulder by a Ryan fastball.

Number six is Dara Torres, a five time Olympic swimmer, who after having a child and coming out of retirement for the second time, won two silver medals at the 2008 Olympic games at the age forty-one. In winning the silver medal in the 50-meter freestyle event, she set a new American record, finishing only one-hundredth of a second behind the winner, twenty-five year old Britta Steffen. Even eight years earlier when she won five Olympic medals, she was the oldest person on the American Olympic swimming team.

Number five is Yuichiro Miura, Japanese mountain climber, a three-time record holder as the oldest person to conquer Mount Everest. He first achieved this feat at age seventy, repeated it five years later, and set the current record at the age of eighty years, 224 days. Honorable mention goes to Shailendra Kumar Upadhyaya, Nepalese politician, who was determined at age eighty-two to break Miura's record or die trying. He did the latter.

Dawn Brooke is number four. The English woman , much to her shock and surprise, had a baby without medical intervention at age fifty-nine, becoming history's oldest known "natural" mother. Honorable mention goes to unmarried Spaniard Maria del Carmen Bousada, who one week shy of her sixty-seventh birthday became the oldest woman to give birth with donated eggs and sperm and plenty of medical help. When accused of being selfish and irresponsible for having children so late in life, she responded that her mother had lived to age 101, so she might even be around long enough to see her grandchildren. She died less than three years later, leaving her twin sons orphaned.

Number three is Jack LaLanne, fitness fanatic and motivational speaker, who at age seventy became the oldest man (and likely the *only* man) to swim a mile towing seventy rowboats while handcuffed and shackled. His attention to fitness seems to have paid off though, as he lived in exceptional health and vigor to age ninety-six.

At number two we have Fauja Singh, British distance runner extraordinaire, was the first (and so far only) hundred-year-old to complete a marathon. Sometimes called the Turbaned Tornado, Singh is a Sikh from Punjab, India who took up running rather late in life after he moved to England, finishing his first marathon at age eighty-nine. With a killer grin and wry sense of humor, he started a London running club called *Sikhs in the City*. At this writing, Mr. Singh is 110 years old, still active, although retired from competitive running, at least for now.

Samuel Whittemore heads my list for his actions at the beginning of the American Revolutionary War. On April 19, 1775 as British troops were retreating toward Boston after the battles of Lexington and Concord, Whittemore heard word of those skirmishes, grabbed a brace of pistols and his musket, and headed out to join the battle. An old soldier who had fought in multiple battles against the French and Indians, Whittemore leapt from behind a fence as the Redcoats approached and shot three of them dead at pointblank range. Unable to reload before the surviving soldiers reached him, he was shot in the face, beaten with musket butts, bayoneted thirteen times, and left for dead. That he survived at all would have been remarkable enough, but even more remarkable, he was eighty years old at the time! After recovering, Whittemore became a local celebrity and went on to live another eighteen years, dying in bed more peacefully than he had lived. To put his accomplishment in perspective, life expectancy in Massachusetts at the time for those not shot, musket-thumped, or bayoneted was about thirty-five years. Today on the Arlington, Massachusetts village green, where the action occurred, there is a monument to Samuel Whittemore. Who can doubt that he deserves it?

Why Sixty-Five?

URING the 2020 election season, I was besieged with reporters asking me what I thought about having the two oldest Presidential nominees ever. Anytime election season is upon us is a good time to remember the quote from the nineteenth century German statesman, Otto von Bismarck. "People never lie so much as after a hunt, during a war, or before an election." Bismarck was clearly not familiar with fishing. He did come up with more than just witticisms though. He invented retirement, something for which you might thank him or curse him, depending on your age and circumstances.

By retirement, of course, I mean government-funded pensions and health care, which allowed people the possibility of not working until they dropped as people had done throughout human history. But at what age should people begin receiving these benefits? In 1890 Bismarck backed a retirement age of seventy, a time of life when he felt most people were "disabled from work by age." As most work was physically demanding in the nineteenth century and life expectancy in Germany at the time was only thirty-nine years, his government was not going to be on the hook for a fortune.

The American Social Security system is now eighty-seven years old. At its beginning during the Great Depression, Social Security benefits became available at age sixty-five. There was no obvious reason for picking that age except that a number of private pensions were already using it at the time. Since 1935 though, the age for full Social Security benefits has crept up by only a year and a half. Age sixty-five is also when you become eligible for Medicare, which itself is now fifty-seven years old. Now, as both Social

Security and Medicare are in various stages of financial difficulty, do these ages still make sense as the time at which people qualify for full old-age benefits? Will doing so break the bank?

I'm a scientist and I don't pretend to have any special insight into complicated policy issues, and the official age of retirement is certainly that. However, it might make sense to begin a conversation on this difficult issue by admitting a little uncontroversial demographic perspective. To begin with, a young person just entering the work force is now more than twice as likely to survive long enough to qualify for benefits as a worker in 1935 when Social Security began. Life expectancy has risen by more than seventeen years since Social Security pensions became available, which not only means that people are more likely to survive long enough to begin receiving benefits now, but also that they are likely to receive them for much longer. Life expectancy at age sixty-five then was about seven years less than it is today. In fact, the life expectancy at age sixty-five then was the same as it is at age seventy-five today.

Health, not just survival, has improved dramatically too. Today's sixty-five year old sees better, thanks to better glasses, cataract surgery, and improved treatment for other visual problems, hears better, thanks to improved hearing aids, walks and even jogs better, thanks to better heart and lung health, improved pain medications and joint replacement surgery, and generally feels and functions better than any generation in human history. In the past thirty years, the disability rate among those sixty-five and over has declined by 15 percent per decade and that decline may even be accelerating.

From a health perspective at least, if the sixty-five year old retirement age made sense in 1935, it makes no sense today. The average person age sixty-five today is almost a different species, far healthier in almost every way we can measure, than an average sixty-five year old in 1935. Accordingly, in 2007 the mandatory retirement age for commercial airline pilots was raised from sixty to sixty-five years.

Given these facts, a reasonable starting point for a discussion about retirement age might be to ask *why it shouldn't be raised to at least age seventy now,* given that an average seventy year old today is quite clearly healthier than a sixty-five year old was in 1935. There may be good reasons for keeping the retirement age where it is, but it seems worth some public discussion about what those reasons are. One thing is certain. The nature of work has changed dramatically. The amount of physical labor done in the workplace has fallen so rapidly that a recent scientific paper blamed it for our current obesity epidemic. To be sure, some jobs still require considerable physical strength and gradually wear down the body over time. Any discussion of changes in the retirement age should be sensitive to such issues. Maybe retirement age should be scaled to occupation or to physical health?

As these questions indicate, altering the retirement age would involve dauntingly complex economic, social and political issues. Not all socioeconomic classes, for instance, have shared equally in the health dividend of the past eighty-seven years. Also, we need to be aware of possible conflicts between generations. In the case of airline pilots, the issue created a sharp division between older pilots, who were for the change, and younger pilots, who were against it. However, the tsunami of retiring baby boomers which is sweeping over America and the rest of the industrialized world is likely to force a conversation about the topic sooner than we'd prefer. A demographic perspective is not, nor should it be, the last word on this issue. However, maybe it should be the first word, a starting point for a necessary, if perhaps painful, public conversation.

The Weaker Sex?

URING the late fall of 1846, a group of poorly-equipped, poorly-led, California-bound pioneers devoid of any particular survival skills and already short of food found themselves stranded in the deepening snows of the Sierra Nevada mountains with winter coming on fast. It would be months before rescue—if it arrived at all—was likely. This was the Donner Party, now infamous because they resorted to murder and cannibalism so that some of them could survive.

Although the psychological pressures that led to the cannibalism—even of children—are fascinating almost two centuries later, what interests me about this well-documented catastrophe is who died and who survived. Of the eighty-seven original members (eighty-nine if you count two native American men who joined them late and were themselves eventually murdered and eaten), forty-seven members of the Donner Party survived, most of them women. More than half of the men, but less than one-third of the women, died.

There are many reasons that you could imagine that the women would survive starvation, malnutrition, and cold exposure more successfully than men. They are smaller, so they need less food. They likely started out with more body fat, so they had more stored energy to live on. Maybe they did less physical work than men during the ordeal. Or possibly in the mistaken belief that they were more fragile or through some remnant of old-fashion chivalry, perhaps they received preferential treatment. Maybe, even, they were less averse than the men to cannibalism.

I'd like to suggest something different—that the survival difference was largely biological; that women, even little girls, are simply better designed for survival than men and boys. If true, which I hope to convince you is pretty much beyond doubt, I would like to know why and how it works.

I was thinking of the Donner party after recently reading an analysis of death and survival during other extremely harsh historical events.

It's well known that under normal conditions, women live longer than men virtually everywhere on earth. Less known is that women die at lower rates than men from all the leading causes of death except Alzheimer's disease. In seasonal flu outbreaks, for instance, typically 40-50 percent more men die than women. Women have survived COVID-19 better than men too.

Females also do better under extreme hardship. The Donner party was a small-scale famine. A much larger one was the Ukraine famine of 1932-33. Caused by a combination of repeated droughts and misguided Soviet government policies, between two-and-a-half and four million Ukrainians starved to death that winter. Life expectancy in a single year fell to just over seven—yes, I said seven—years for Ukrainian men. It was brutal for women too, but their life expectancy was more than three years longer.

Similarly, during a severe famine in Sweden during 1773, life expectancy for men plummeted to seventeen years. Life expectancy for women was two years longer. During the seven year Irish Potato famine in the mid-nineteenth century, starvation and its malnutrition-related diseases would kill more than a million mostly poor Irishmen. Once again, the bigger toll was on men, whose life expectancy fell by more than twenty years over that time. Women suffered as well, but their life expectancy "only" fell by sixteen years.

Surprisingly, in all of these national famines, the difference between male and female life expectancy was mostly due to better survival of baby girls compared to baby boys. Adult women survived better than men, but the difference was considerably smaller than among babies.

Women not only survive famine better, they survive disease epidemics better too. Today, we think of measles as a relatively mild disease, largely because childhood vaccinations have made it rare. Also because after many generations of exposure to it, we developed some collective resistance to its worst effects. When it strikes populations with no previous exposure though, measles can be devastating. It killed two-thirds of the native population of Cuba when they were first exposed in 1529, for instance, as well as half the population of Honduras. The same year the Donner party was starving in the Sierras, a measles epidemic tore through the isolated population of

Iceland, killing 80 percent of newborn girls. Female life expectancy fell to nineteen years. But the epidemic killed almost 90 percent of newborn boys. Male life expectancy dropped even further—to seventeen years.

An even worse fate met a group of about fifteen thousand freed American slaves and their descendants when they voluntarily migrated to what is now Liberia over a twenty year period in the early nineteenth century.

The American Colonization Society or ACS, a strange alliance of abolitionists and slave owners, organized the migration and kept records of the migrants' fate. Although these migrants were all of African ancestry, they had no recent exposure to a whole range of tropical diseases. Upon arrival, they died at unprecedented rates. According to ACS records, only 5 percent of newborn boys survived to age five whereas about 8 percent of girls lived to that age. Overall, life expectancy of the newly arrived migrants was only an incredible eighteen months for the men, but it was a little more than two years for the women.

To what is this greater female hardiness due? To tell the truth, we simply don't know. Suspicion has fallen on hormones, of course. Some kind of toxic effect of testosterone, perhaps? In the first year of life, boy babies do have a spike in testosterone that then goes away again until puberty, when it roars back. Interestingly, a previous study of the royal court in Korea over a three century period found that eunuchs—castrated men, who were the only men outside the royal family allowed to stay in the palace overnight—lived about twenty years longer than the uncastrated men in the court.

Whatever the reason, women and girls seem to be the tougher, more resilient, sex. When things get tough, men are, comparatively speaking, wimps. Whatever is responsible for that, we men would like to share a little of it. Please.

No Fool Like an Old Fool?

ECENT events in the entertainment world and elsewhere have many people wondering whether old men in positions of power are compelled to behave foolishly. Does growing old mean having your judgment corrupted if not obliterated? On the other hand, weren't we all taught that age is supposed to confer wisdom and sound judgment?

Raymond Pearl, a pioneer in the study of human aging, had no doubts. He was firmly in the aged-equals-foolish camp. In fact, Pearl thought that people should be ineligible to vote after age fifty because their judgment would be so clouded. A man of strong, idiosyncratic, and often spectacularly wrong opinions, he was also convinced that exercise was harmful to your health. He thought this because he noticed that lawyers and accountants lived longer than coal miners. What else could that be due to than coal miners getting more physical exercise?

In 1927 Pearl even published a newspaper article called "Why Lazy People Live the Longest." Pearl himself strenuously avoided physical, although not mental, exercise. During his life he published seventeen books and more than seven hundred scientific papers, not to mention innumerable magazine and newspaper articles, before dying of a heart attack at age sixty-one, something that may have been prevented or delayed, as we know now, by a little exercise.

Real connoisseurs of human judgment, scam artists, would seem to agree with Pearl. Crime statistics indicate quite clearly that they preferentially target seniors, no doubt because experience teaches them that they will be most successful at separating seniors from their money. The FBI even has a special web page devoted to senior citizens as targets of fraud.

Consistent with this evidence, a recent study found that about one-quarter of people age in their late sixties reported having difficulty managing their finances and that increased to more than two-thirds of people by age eighty-five.

Part of the reason for the increase in susceptibility to fraud with age may be that aging brings with it an increased frequency of various forms of dementia. By age eighty-five, an age that more than 40 percent of Americans now reach, about one-third of us will have some form of dementia. It may be that people in the early stages of dementing diseases are the ones most easily duped by con men. Another possibility is that as people get older and their bodies begin to fail them, they become more reliant on others for help and thus become more trusting and less discerning about whom they should trust.

On the other hand, we have people like ninety-one year old Warren Buffet who continues to be one of the most successful investors on earth and a host of other seniors whose brains are clearly anything but addled.

Respect for the wisdom of the elderly is as old as human history. In ancient Sparta twenty-five hundred years ago, a governing body called the *gerousia* required that a man (of course, a man) had to be at least sixty years old to be a member. This was a time when surviving sixty years of war, pestilence, and palace intrigue was no small feat and probably involved considerable guile and wit as well as luck. So that age limit may have been justifiable.

In our own Congress, a wise body in theory if not in practice, things haven't changed much since ancient Sparta. Average age of House members just before the 2018 election was fifty-seven years and of Senators was sixty-one years, and that's the youngest Congress has been in a while.

As we age, there is no question that our ability to do certain kinds of mental gymnastics declines. Chess champions don't tend to stay champions beyond their thirties or forties. We get worse with age at recalling the details of a long paragraph we read a few hours ago. We also don't do as well at remembering names or various "naming" tasks. That is, if someone asks you to name as many animals or vegetables or words beginning with the letter "F," for instance, in a minute, the number of names you can come up with decreases as you age.

But who cares whether you can still beat your children or grandchildren in chess or how many animals you can name in a minute compared with important things like making reasoned judgments about life?

Wisdom, the ability to observe and sensibly evaluate problems of real life, is one of the few things that doesn't seem to decline with age—at least in those without brain disease. Some studies even find that it increases. This may have to do with older people having more, and broader, life experiences, not being in a hurry to reach decisions, developing an ability to think about problems from multiple perspectives.

Is there anything we can do to help preserve our mental acuity as we age?

A few years ago I attended a national "Cognitive Aging Summit," an august scientific conference where this issue came up repeatedly. There was not much enthusiasm among the experts for the effectiveness of the many brain games currently on the market. However, a surprisingly consistent finding was that staying physically active seems to help preserve brain function. Physical exercise turns out to be good not just for your heart, bones, muscles, and lungs. It's good for your brain too. Too bad Raymond Pearl isn't around to hear this.

In contrast to Pearl consider the attitude of Noah Webster—American revolutionary, author, editor, and dictionary maker. Webster felt that it was the young who were foolish. People should be *deprived* of the right to vote until they were at least age forty-five, he said, and no one should be eligible to hold an important public office until he was at least age fifty. Growing older certainly did not make him foolish. He published his famous dictionary at age seventy and continued improving and revising it until virtually the day he fell over for good at age eighty-four.

So who's right, Pearl or Webster? Somehow I suspect one's answer might depend on one's age.

The Blue Zone Myth

W E all long for Shangri-La, a place of endless tranquility, loving families and friends, hard, honest work, and long, healthy lives. Actually, not everyone longs for that. It sounds like the most boring possible place to me. The long, healthy life part sounds pretty good though.

Enough people long for Shangri-La though, that descriptions of supposedly real places just like it, along with the secrets of their exceptional health and longevity, have become a recognizable media genre. The original, clearly fictional, Shangri-La was described in James Hilton's 1933 novel *Lost Horizon* as lying in a remote mountain valley "far beyond the Western Himalayas." So, more recent Shangri-La's are most often in remote mountain valleys. Remote islands are acceptable as well.

One of the pioneers of what might be called reality-based, unintentional fiction was Dr. Donald Davies of the Medical College of London, a specialist in aging, who set out in the late 1960's to discover whether rumors of such places were true, and if so, what were their secrets of longevity. He visited—where else?—the western Himalayas. He also spent a few days in the Soviet Caucasus Mountains, where people claimed to live as long as one hundred fifty or even one hundred sixty years. But he was most intrigued with the valley of Vilcabamba in the Ecuadorean Andes, probably because it was the safest and easiest of these places to visit repeatedly. His 1975 book (*The Centenarians of the Andes*) makes for some knee-slapping reading today. He attributes the long lives of the Vilcabambans to their positive attitude, hard work, sparse diet, and some trace minerals in the soil. Other aspects of life in Vilcabamba wouldn't appear to be all that health-promoting. They smoked and drank alcohol extravagantly. At times of stress, he reports, "the males drink themselves into a stupor; they also do this regularly on weekends." Yet it is the men of Vilcabamba who were supposedly long-lived.

The story of Vilcabamba has long ago been debunked as a product of local illiteracy, poor birth records, and erratic memories of the older people. However such stories live on today. Such areas have been called by journalist Dan Buettner, "Blue Zones." Do such places really exist and can we learn anything new about good health habits from studying them?

Clusters of long-lived healthy people, say, those living to age one hundred and over, certainly do exist. Sometimes they even exist in remote mountain valleys or islands. The question is why?

One answer might be genes. We know that genes play a considerable role in exceptional health and longevity (although they play less a role in more normal longevity). People living on islands and in remote mountain villages usually don't move far from where they were born. After a while, there are no people around to marry who aren't fairly close relatives. So if by chance, a longevity-promoting gene cropped up in one of these villages, because of higher than normal inbreeding, it might soon spread among a lot of the local people. A longevity cluster is born.

Another answer might be luck, or as I call it, the blue marble effect. If you take a box full of thousands of different colored marbles and sling them across the floor, somewhere in that mess you are likely to find a cluster of mostly blue (and somewhere else brown or yellow) marbles. It's chance. But if you didn't know that someone had slung the marbles randomly, you might ask yourself what was it about that particular spot that made those blue marbles cluster there?

The third, and I think least likely, possibility is that people in certain areas have discovered uniquely healthy lifestyles. This would be easy to check, although people searching for the secrets of longevity never do so. Scientists call it a control group. Just hike your way five miles down the road to where the neighbors don't claim to be living so long and find out if they live pretty much the same lifestyle. I bet they do.

Besides, the secret of healthy life isn't really a secret. Don't eat too much, eat plenty of fruits and veggies, don't smoke, drink in moderation, get plenty of exercise, don't skydive without a parachute or ride a motorcycle without a helmet.

There, I've saved you twenty-five dollars on the next "secrets of longevity" book.

When Would you Like to Stop Aging?

I HAVE a pill, a super vitamin, I mean a *really* super vitamin. If you decide to take my pill, you immediately stop aging and are preserved in your current physical state from this day forward. Would you take it? What if you could go back in time and take it at any age? What age would you choose?

This hypothetical pill that stops aging, call it the Methuselah pill, will not make you immortal. Immortality does not exist in this world, if for no other reason than freak accidents are inevitable given enough time. Whether or not you age, you can still step in front of a bus, eat a contaminated hamburger, catch a stray bullet, or be struck by lightning. In fact, if you lived long enough one of these things would almost be guaranteed to happen to you.

One way that scientists define aging is that it increases the chance that you will die in the coming year. Remember, in America, your chance of dying during the next year doubles about every eight years after age thirty-five. But with the Methuselah pill that no longer happens. You have the same chance of dying, you look the same, you feel the same, as the age at which you took the pill, forever. Would you want to be frozen in time with the physical looks, the energy, mental prowess, strength and agility you had when you were twenty? Give this some careful thought because half of you, the male half, may remember twenty as the testosterone-soaked age at which you were more than a little crazy. Maybe you'd like to be preserved at age fifty, when people take you more seriously. You would be more settled in life, a bit more thoughtful perhaps, but a bit less swift or agile.

One thing to consider. The age you choose to stop aging has a great deal to do with how much longer you can expect to live. Remember, you're not immortal. You survive at the rate that people the age at which you took the pill survive. It's just that the rate never changes. Here is where the numbers become fun.

Say you liked being a testosterone-laden male and decide to stop aging on your twentieth birthday. A little simple algebra with U.S. government statistics shows that with a twenty year old male survival rate lasting into infinity, your life expectancy is roughly another six hundred years rather than the fifty-seven additional years it is in reality. Not a bad bargain for staying a little crazy.

If you're a woman, you're not so crazy at that age and you are also better designed for survival than your male counterparts. That's a sad fact of biology, men. Women could expect to survive another seventeen hundred years rather than the normal sixty-two years of additional life in our current reality. Notice, this is nearly three times as long as those crazy men. I know it doesn't sound fair, fellows, but age twenty is when the survival advantage of women over men is close to its greatest.

If you decided to stop aging instead when you are a dignified, thoughtful, and mature fifty year-old, you will have sacrificed a lot of future years to achieve that dignified look. Fifty year olds are about six times more likely to die in a given year than twenty year olds. Not only that, but you could expect to live with some aches and pains that you didn't anticipate. You won't hear as well and will probably be holding the newspaper or your smart phone at arm's length, but at least that testosterone problem will no longer be so pressing. Your life expectancy now, however, has dropped to a mere one hundred forty additional years if you're a man and a little over two hundred years if you're a woman. Ladies, that decision to stop aging at fifty rather than twenty has now cost you fifteen hundred years of life expectancy and a considerable amount of pain. You suspected it was a bad decision, didn't you?

The point of this exercise, I suppose, besides having a little fun and stimulating a little thought is to give readers a visceral feel for the toll that aging exacts on us. Back here in the real world, there has been only one person, Jeanne Calment, in the history of our species who is confirmed to have lived at least one hundred and twenty years. No one yet has approached one hundred thirty years, although some of us researchers are working to change that.

If you really want to have a long life though, you'd take the Methuselah pill at age ten— and of course be a girl. At age ten, life, as I faintly remember it, is simple. Your biggest problems are managing your social relations and your parents. Your parents shouldn't be a long-term problem, because you could now expect to live a vampire-like eighty-seven hundred years.

Ah, to be ten again.

Young Blood, I Can't Get You Out of my Mind

COULD it be that Count Dracula was on to something after all? Dracula, at least the movie version of him, drinks the blood of young, beautiful people so that he can remain young, beautiful, and immortal. His victims are transformed as well. They can stay young, beautiful and immortal too, as long as *they* can find enough blood meals from their as-yet-unbitten young and beautiful friends. I guess the "immortal" part may not be technically correct. The appropriate term seems to be "undead," but that looks to me a lot like "alive," just with a craving for young blood.

As with all medications, there are side effects of drinking young blood if you are a vampire. First, you have to avoid sunlight forever after. But let's face it, sunlight ages skin. This is called photo-aging by dermatologists. So becoming a vampire can be said to improve skin health. Vampires also apparently have excellent dental health even if they develop a bit of an overbite. One problem the movies don't emphasize enough is how difficult staying well-groomed is for vampires. With no mirror reflection, doing your hair or touching up that eyeliner probably gives a vampire fits.

All kidding aside, young blood may indeed turn out to have fountain-of-youth-like properties for us just as it apparently had for Dracula. That's what some intriguing mouse experiments tell us.

The mouse experiments I am talking about work like this. Two mice are surgically sewn together side-by-side. The blood vessels underlying the surgical site on each mouse will grow together and fuse. They now share a single blood supply.

Although this technique has been used in the laboratory for more than a hundred and fifty years, don't try it at home, folks. It only works with laboratory mice that are genetically identical to one another. If the mice were genetically different they would both die from a massive immune rejection of one another.

What scientists hadn't done until relatively recently was to suture an old mouse to a young mouse and observe how that affected both of them. As we all know, the older you get, the slower you heal if injured. So researchers injured a muscle of the older mouse of these old-young conjoined pairs and found that the old muscle healed like the mouse was much younger. There appeared to be something in the young blood that was making the old muscles act like they were young again.

Other labs followed suit, checking out whether young blood could rejuvenate old mouse hearts. It could. Others investigated the brain. Could young blood improve memory in an aging brain? It could. What this might mean of course is that there is something in young mouse blood that is rejuvenating.

Researchers don't often mention the other result. The muscle, heart, and brain of the younger mouse in the old-young pair appeared to grow older. So maybe there is something in the blood of old mice that accelerated aging.

Here is where it begins to get spooky. Researchers transfused the blood—actually only the plasma, the liquid part of the blood—of young *humans* into old *mice*. The memory of the old mice improved. Whatever rejuvenation factors were in young mouse blood was apparently there in human blood too.

No, they didn't sew a mouse to a human or vice versa. In this case, they used traditional hypodermic needles for the transfusing. Take note, normal human blood would kill a normal mouse because of the immune response. They had to use a mouse with its immune system removed to do this experiment.

One of the problems with this sort of rejuvenation research is that people are so desperate to remain young that at the slightest hint of scientific progress in that direction, long before there is clear proof, some people will be willing to pay to give whatever it is a try.

Before long, as you might expect, a company arose that would top you up with plasma from someone of college age for a hefty price. They claimed to be doing science, tracking their customers for signs of improved health. The FDA didn't buy it and shut them down. Research continues though and if the promise from mouse research extends to people, you will no doubt hear about it.

I was thinking of this the other day walking around my own college campus, noticing signs all over advertising pay for plasma donation. Blood plasma has all sorts of valuable products in it for producing pharmaceuticals. In fact, plasma donation is now an eleven billion dollar industry. This, by the way, is an industry in which America is still number one. About 70 percent of all worldwide plasma donations come from the USA.

Of course, college students and other down-and-outers do not get rich donating plasma. I went through this thoroughly unpleasant experience several times as a graduate student, getting as I recall, about twenty dollars per donation and I could donate every two weeks. I think the going rate currently is more like fifty dollars per donation.

Where some people see exploitation, others see a business opportunity. College students listen up. There are people out there—lots of them—who are willing to pay thousands of dollars for a transfusion of your plasma. How does this compare with the fifty dollars every two weeks you may be making as a plasma donor now?

Vampires don't have to be the only blood suckers out there.

VIII.

A Bit of This and That

One of Eight Billion—
Aren't You Special?

F RETTING about the economy? COVID-19? Global warming? Your children's future? Your own future? Time to put you—and your problems—in perspective.

You are only one of about eight billion people on this planet. While that is an easy number to write, neither you nor I can grasp it easily.

Our brains evolved to deal with small numbers to solve immediate problems. How many lions were in that group that was stalking me? How many mouths do I have to feed tomorrow? Is my clan bigger than my neighbor's? Questions like these can be answered by grasping numbers not much bigger than you can count on your fingers and toes.

We need help to grasp bigger numbers.

For instance, think of the most star-filled sky you've ever seen. Clear, moonless, no intruding city lights, the widest horizon possible. The Milky Way glistens. How many stars are you looking at? Millions? How many millions? Actually, you are seeing only a couple of thousand stars at best.

This is how badly our gut instincts mislead us about big numbers.

So how can we grasp the number of other people who share our planet, many of them with problems much, much worse than yours?

Analogies sometimes work. For instance, if you stacked up eight billion nickels, one for each person on earth, that stack would reach nearly eight thousand miles high. If you built your stack of nickels in New York City and it fell over, American coins could shower down on Calcutta.

Getting back to your problems, the philosopher and mathematician Bertrand Russell once said that a good cure for human self-importance is a little astronomy.

Let's see.

All eight billion of us live on a medium size planet orbiting a medium size star in a medium size galaxy in a largely empty universe. We are now exploring more of our universe, for instance sending the New Horizons space probe whirling through space to investigate the recently-demoted, dwarf planet Pluto in the outer reaches of our solar system. We're pretty proud of our success as we should be. That journey took nearly ten years. New Horizons, zipping along at more than forty thousand miles per hour, travelled a total of about three billion miles and hit the bull's-eye. That's pretty impressive all right.

Three billion miles is so far away that radio signals, traveling at the speed of light, took about four-and-a-half hours to reach us from Pluto. Light, in case you forgot, takes only a little more than a second to travel from earth to the moon.

But our solar system is a drop of water in the ocean of the universe. If New Horizons continued on (as it has) at the same speed, it would take ninety thousand years to reach the closest star. Put another way, if you shrunk the universe down until our sun was the size of a nickel, the closest star would be four hundred miles from it.

See what I mean? Nearly empty.

And that's just the closest star in one galaxy—our Milky Way Galaxy— which is estimated to contain at least one hundred billion other stars plus at least that many planets that like earth have climates potentially capable of harboring life. So maybe there are people—or something—on a few billion or so of those planets all thinking about their own problems.

All those stars and all that emptiness take up a lot of space, so to speak. Our galaxy is so big that it takes a ray of light more than a hundred thousand years to cross it.

The biggest question, literally, then is how many *galaxies* are there in the universe? Estimating from what we can see with the Hubble space telescope, the lowball number is about a hundred billion, and the highball number as of today, is about ten trillion galaxies. There is no point writing out all those zeros. They would be pretty meaningless. We've apparently come a long ways since we all did our counting on our fingers and toes.

But try this. Scientists in Hawaii with clearly too much time on their hands worked up an estimate of the total number of grains of sand on earth—on all the beaches, on all the dunes, on all the deserts and the sea bottom. Everywhere. I won't bother to give you that estimate, but if those Hawaiian scientists are in the right ballpark, then it would take all grains of sand from all those beaches, dunes, sea bottoms, and deserts on at least ten thousand earths similar to our own to equal the lowest estimate of the number of stars in the universe.

So there you are. One of eight billion people on a planet orbiting a star that in the total scheme of things is less than what a single grain of sand would be to ten thousand earths. How important do your troubles seem now?

In the famous last line from the movie *Casablanca*, Humphrey Bogart sums things up nicely when he says "It doesn't take much to see that the problems of three little people don't amount to a hill of beans in this crazy world." Okay, maybe he should have said "this crazy *universe*" instead. But as usual, Bogey had a point.

Metric, Please

So a twelve stone bloke walks into a pub, orders a pint, and plops down ten bob.

Unless you spent some time in England prior to 1970, or have read more than your share of old English novels, that previous sentence may be a bit obscure.

The reason is that the Brits used to pride themselves on the obscurity of their system of weights, measures, and currency.

Let me translate that first sentence. A stone, when used to describe a person, is fourteen pounds. That's pounds as in weight, not pounds as in money. So the bloke weighs 168 pounds. A pint? Well, you probably think you know what a pint is, but we will see if you really do when we return to that shortly. A bob is British slang for a shilling. Before decimalization of their currency in 1971, a British shilling was worth twelve pence and twenty shillings made a pound (money, not weight). So a pound was two hundred and forty pence.

Are you following me, because now it begins to get complicated? A florin was two shillings, a crown five shillings, a guinea twenty-one shillings, that is a pound plus a shilling.

I used to think that the British did these things just so they could fleece tourists or at least make Americans feel stupid. But I've now decided that our system of weights and measures is at least as crazy, particularly as we are the only industrialized country that refuses to go metric.

Consider that pint back in the first sentence. In the U.S. we have pints too. We inherited our system of weights and measures from the British, so you might expect that they would be the same. They are not. The U.S. pint is 20 percent less than a British pint, 473 milliliters (to bring in a rationale unit of liquid measure into the conversation) compared to 568 milliliters. In both England and the U.S. a gallon is eight pints, so American gallons are about 20 percent smaller than American gallons.

We have inches, feet, yards and miles. Twelve inches to a foot, three feet to a yard, 1760 yards to a mile. And then there are those quaint measures of the horsey set, the hand is four inches and a furlong is 220 yards. Our measure of land area is the acre, which as we all know is equivalent to the area enclosed by a rectangle one furlong in length and one-tenth of a furlong (a chain, that is) wide. Are you telling me British currency is crazy? Maybe it was, but at least they've changed it.

Don't even get me started on ounces.

Okay, I'm started. In America we use ounces in two ways, one way measures volume (a fluid ounce), the other measure weight (an avoirdupois ounce). Usually, we ignore this difference and if you're measuring water, they are pretty much the same. However, for other substances, such as flour for instance, one type of ounce is about twice as much as the other. Of course, British ounces and American ounces are different too.

The advantage of the metric system is that it makes intuitive sense. It is based on ten's and decimals like our numbers. Like our fingers and toes. You have grams, meters, and liters. Put a prefix, milli-, cent-, deci-, in front of any of them and it means one-thousandth, one-hundredth, or one-tenth, respectively. For those of us in the sciences who often work at smaller levels, there is also micro- and nano-, a millionth- and a billionth-. Kilo- means one thousand. Instead of the chain-by-furlong acre, the metric system has the hectare, equivalent to the area of a square one hundred meters on a side.

Thankfully, Alexander Hamilton made our currency sensible in 1792 when the *Coinage Act* officially established the dollar. Originally, the dollar was based on the considerably less sensible Spanish dollar, also known as a "piece of eight" as it was worth eight *reales*. We still have a vestige of that original Spanish dollar in our all-but-vanished unit of bits, which were also eight to the dollar. "Two bits, four bits, six bits, a dollar," as the jingle went. I remember as a boy my father telling me that something cost six bits and having no idea what he was talking about. Other than that though, we have a nice pseudo-metric monetary system. A dollar consists of ten dimes and one hundred cents. In Hamilton's day there was also an eagle coin worth ten dollars and a mille, worth one-thousandth of a dollar, that is one-tenth of a cent. You wonder what could be bought with a mille?

It has worked well with our money, which is now the international currency of choice, so can we please all go metric as the French did in 1799 and science also did long ago? Actually, as *almost* all science did long ago. You might recall that in 1999 NASA sent a one hundred and twenty-five million dollar weather orbiter crashing into the Martian surface because one of the two teams of engineers working on the navigation system was using the metric system, the other was using so-called English measures. That's an expensive lesson on why we all need to go metric. The sooner, the better.

We Are on the Move

No matter how still you sit, or how intensely you focus on not twitching a finger, scratching an itch, or blinking an eye, you cannot help moving very, very fast

For starters, if you are sitting on the equator, you are moving from west to east at about a thousand miles per hour as the earth rotates on its axis.

Even if you are sitting at the North Pole, where you would not be moving so much as rotating very slowly in one spot, you would still be zipping right along, because the earth itself is orbiting the sun at sixty-five thousand miles per hour. And the sun itself along with our whole solar system is slowly orbiting around the massive black hole at the center of our Milky Way galaxy.

When I say "slowly" orbiting I mean that only with respect to how long it takes our solar system to complete an orbit around the galaxy. In this case, a single orbit takes roughly two hundred and thirty million years. The last time we were at this point in our galactic orbit, the first dinosaurs were just about to appear on earth. The next time, if history is any guide, humans will be long gone and some other life form will be dominating our planet.

Our galactic orbit is huge, so completing it in only two hundred and thirty million years requires that we get a move on. We are orbiting our galaxy at about five hundred thousand miles per hour, more than fast enough to muss your hair if our atmosphere weren't moving at the same speed with you.

The movement that really interests me today though is much slower than any of these. It is one to two inches per year. That is about the rate at which fingernails grow and also about the rate at which continents slide over the earth.

Movement of continents, and the openings and closings of oceans because of that movement, were first described in detail by German physicist-astronomer-meteorologist and polar adventurer Alfred Wegener in 1912. Wegener was one of those scientists who contributed to so many scientific fields that it is difficult to describe him without a long series of hyphenated nouns.

Wegener's biggest and most lasting contribution to science, however, was the idea that continents move around on the face of the earth like ice cubes floating in a punch bowl. This was one of those ideas like Darwin's idea of natural selection that was brilliantly simple and yet explained so much.

Prior to Wegener, oceans and mountains were assumed to be caused by crinkling of the earth's surface as the earth gradually cooled from a molten beginning, something like the skin of a baked apple wrinkles after you take it out of the oven. The wrinkled apple scenario explained very little though except maybe why there might be mountains and oceans in the first place. It didn't explain, for instance, why mountains are so often found along the edges of continents.

Some features of the earth were difficult to attribute to a wrinkled skin. The Pacific Ocean, for instance, is so large and deep that it was thought to have formed when a chunk of earth burst loose and flew into space, becoming our moon and leaving behind a giant seawater-filled crater. George Darwin, Charles's son, championed this notion.

But Wegener made it all exquisitely simple. He noticed as many school children, and even some professional geologists, had before him that the east coast of South America and the west Coast of Africa could easily fit together like pieces of a jigsaw puzzle. Wegener also knew that sea level had risen and fallen by hundreds of feet over time, so that current coastlines could be misleading. But he noticed too that the edges of the recently-discovered continental shelves fit together even better than current coastlines. Once he fully accepted that continents could move, a new reality snapped into place.

That new reality explained why the same fossils were found along the western coast of Africa and the eastern coast of South America. It was because those continents had once been joined and then split apart. It explained why fossils of tropical species could be found in polar regions.

It explained why the composition of rocks that formed the Appalachian Mountains, the mountains of eastern Greenland, of Scotland, and of Scandinavia was so similar. At one time, they formed a single mountain chain on a single continent.

Mountain ranges, volcanoes, not to mention earthquakes, were so often found along the edges of continental shelves because they were all due to the geological mayhem created when continental plates crashed into one another, yes, at the blinding speed at which fingernails grow.

We can see this happening now along the west coast of South America, where the oceanic Nazca plate is pushing its way under the South American plate causing earthquakes and volcanic eruptions while thrusting the Andes higher and higher. The Himalayas are also growing as India, once a separate continent, continues its migration north, slowly pushing its way into the rest of Asia like a tomahawk head pressing into flesh.

Maybe the most remarkable result of Wegener's "continental drift" theory was that despite the many geological puzzles it solved so simply, it was almost universally rejected by geologists of his time.

There are at least three reasons for this, which can teach us a bit about the dynamics of scientific progress.

First, Wegener committed the sin of not being trained as a geologist. Experts do not like to be told they are wrong by smarty pants outsiders, even if the outsiders have the evidence on their side.

Second, scientists are a skeptical lot by temperament and training. They prefer to hang on to prevailing orthodoxies because those orthodoxies represent the accumulated knowledge they absorbed during their training. To replace the prevailing orthodoxy of inherently skeptical scientists requires a mountain of convincing evidence. Wegener's evidence had a fatal flaw. He could not identify any plausible force that could be powering the movement of earth's plates. It took another forty years to detect seafloor spreading, caused by molten rock welling up from the earth's mantle. With this knowledge in hand even the geologists had to concede that Wegener had been right.

By the way, note that long-time climate scientists have leapt *en masse* aboard the human-caused climate change express. That should tell you something about the power of the evidence. It has been widely quickly accepted even by habitually skeptical scientists who know and understand the evidence better than anyone.

Finally, Wegener was fatally attracted to polar adventures and like so many polar explorers met a premature death, in his case, on a Greenland ice sheet. Dead scientists do not make energetic, persistent, or convincing advocates for their ideas.

In the end though, Wegener was right. In science, that's all that ultimately counts.

Is There Such a Thing as Sea Level?

A FEW years back while visiting Israel, I found myself bobbing like a cork in the Dead Sea which a nearby sign told me was the lowest place on earth, 420 meters (or 1,378 feet) below sea level. The Dead Sea is well-known for being one of the saltiest bodies of water in the world, almost ten times as salty as the ocean. You could probably float an anvil in it.

As I floated there in salty silence, one thing began bothering me. What in the world does "sea level" really mean? Is the earth really like a giant bath tub filled with water to an easily defined level?

The more I thought about it, I realized this was about more than just the Dead Sea. Mountain heights are also defined by sea level. Mount Everest is reputedly 8,848 meters (29,029 feet) above sea level. What exactly does that mean?

The first thing you have to accept, and it's not that easy once you start thinking about it, is that such a thing as sea level, zero depth (or height) you might call it, actually exists.

We know that the height of the sea surface changes all the time. It changes minute by minute as tides rise and fall. It changes day by day as the moon's gravitational influence waxes and wanes. It changes seasonally with variation in water temperature, salinity, the direction of ocean currents, the size of waves, and a number of other things. Looking closely at the Dead Sea shoreline as I floated there, it was pretty obvious that its level had changed—fallen—recently too. I bet myself that the negative 420 meter sign was no longer accurate, assuming that it had been at some time in the recent past.

A seemingly straightforward approach to defining sea level might be to repeatedly measure where the sea surface touches the same immoveable object such as a wharf or bridge piling. The average level of those measures could be called sea level, then the height (or depth) of everything else could be calculated relative to this "zero point." You might even do this formally with some sort of measuring rod instead of a wharf piling. I call this the stick-in-the-mud technique for measuring sea level. It might seem crude by modern standards, but in fact that pretty closely describes how it is actually done.

But here is a problem. When you do that, you find that sea level differs depending upon where you measure it.

In the late nineteenth century, the world's scientists fixed such problems of measurement by simply agreeing on a single standard for, say, measuring latitude and longitude, time, length, weight, and so on.

But sea level for some reason has never been standardized.

The standard for individual countries is pretty arbitrary in fact. For instance, sea level in England is a stick-in-the-mud measurement made at one point along the western British coast during World War I. Measured at the same spot today, the sea averages eight inches higher than it did back then. But the British, resolute as always, stick to this World War I standard. Germany naturally uses a different standard, measured at Amsterdam. The French measure theirs at Marseilles, where the sea turns out to be nineteen inches lower than the British standard.

There are around a hundred such sea level standards currently in use. So I'm more suspicious than ever about the exactitude of the elevation of the Dead Sea, Mount Everest, or anything else.

Looking at the bigger picture, why do we measure the height or depth of things relative to sea level in the first place?

If we shift our thinking from a sea level perspective, it changes pretty much everything. For instance, instead of calling the Dead Sea the lowest point on earth, we would probably call the Challenger Deep in the Mariana Trench the lowest point. At about seven miles below sea level, we can all agree that it is much lower than the Dead Sea even if you can't float on your back there.

Notice that I still used sea level as a standard. It is devilishly difficult to avoid. Forget about low points. How about high points?

What if instead of using sea level, you calculated mountain heights from their base, the point where the mountain begins to rise up from the surrounding earth? Now, Everest is only about fifteen thousand feet high, an also-ran among tall mountains, and the world's tallest mountain becomes Mauna Kea on Hawaii's big island, which although not quite fourteen thousand feet high *above* the sea actually arises from about twenty thousand feet *below* the sea surface, for a grand total of nearly thirty-four thousand feet, dwarfing Everest and the rest of the Himalayas.

This new calculation could certainly rob summiting the world's highest peak of some of its romantic derring-do allure. Instead of risking death in the ice, avalanches, and oxygen-starved air of Everest, you could drive your car to the top of the world's highest peak.

There is a more sensible, and easily standardized, way to calculate all heights and depths on the earth though.

With modern satellite and other technology, we can now calculate to within about an inch how far anything is from the gravitational center of the earth, which may be thousands of miles beneath our feet, but is without controversy a single well-defined reference point.

The earth it turns out isn't exactly spherical like a basketball. It is squashed toward the center, like a basketball with someone sitting on it. This shape means that the earth is widest at the equator and narrowest from pole-to-pole. Put another way the earth's surface at the equator is farther from the earth's center than anywhere else. From this perspective, mountains get bonus points for height just for being near the equator.

With this new measure, the Dead Sea may still be the lowest point on the global surface at which you can float on your back (or front) without half trying, but the real lowest point is now the ocean, or rather the ice, surface at the North Pole. The South Pole is out of contention because it has more than nine thousand feet of ice piled up on top of the Antarctic continent.

Also from this perspective, Kenya's Mount Kilimanjaro, sitting just south of the equator which is not among the world's tallest one hundred and fifty mountains by traditional standards, becomes the world's sixth tallest.

The new number one is Chimborazo in the Ecuadorian Andes, now over a mile higher than Everest. In fact the top five highest peaks are all in the Andes of either Ecuador or Peru.

From a scientific perspective, I like this measure. It is clean and rigorous. Its use would make the exact determination of sea level of interest mainly to children building sand castles, or adults sleeping on beach towels at the shore. I'm pretty sure that Ecuador and Peru would like it too.

Why Public Opinion Polls Fail

T HE most famously erroneous public opinion poll in American political history is without question the Gallup poll predicting that Thomas Dewey would defeat Harry Truman in the 1948 Presidential election. Mistaken faith in polls that election season led the *Chicago Daily Tribune* to rush into print an edition with the massive head-line "Dewey Defeats Truman" before the actual votes revealed Truman to be the easy four-and-a-half percent winner.

The polls also blew it in the 2016 Brexit election in the United Kingdom. They blew it again, of course, in our 2016 Presidential election. Ironically, at least two of the most respected pollsters in the United States wrote articles in mid-October pointing out why that year's Presidential election would have no "Dewey Defeats Truman"-type surprises. What happened?

Polling is a scientifically sophisticated enterprise, much more scientifically sophisticated today than it was in 1948. Yet, it can obviously still go wrong. If science is, as I believe, still the best way to understand the material world, what flaws underlie these failures?

First off, conspiracy theorists calm down. The 2016 polling errors were no more a conspiracy of the liberal mainstream media than the 2012 election polls that predicted a toss-up (Obama ultimately beat Romney by a comfortable 5 percent) were a conspiracy of the conservative media. It's just that accurate polling, despite its scientific rigor, is getting more and more difficult.

George Gallup introduced real science into polling in 1936 when his upstart polling company correctly predicted that Franklin Roosevelt would win that year's election (which he did easily by 25 percent) whereas a much bigger, better known and more expensive rival poll predicted a landslide win for Roosevelt's opponent, Alf Landon.

Gallup had realized that a representative sample of voters made for better predictions than a large, but possibly biased, sample.

Ironically, Gallup's sampling method had its own problems as the 1948 election revealed. His pollsters were each given quotas of the type of people they had to interview. For instance, one person might be told to interview twelve African-American males in their forties, another to interview twenty Caucasian females in their thirties. The idea is if you choose these quotas carefully, when you combine the results, it will accurately reflect the opinions of the country as a whole.

This might seem like a sensible method, but it can have its own biases, such as if pollsters get their entire quota from, say, in front of a homeless shelter versus a country club. Truly random sampling is actually better. Also, the 1948 polls also made the mistake of stopping two weeks prior to the election. Our 2016 election only confirmed what has been known for a long time. Voters often make up their minds at the last minute.

What about polls today? They are much more sophisticated. Why do they still make major mistakes?

One answer—the answer favored by the pollsters themselves—is that they weren't *really* all that wrong. They might have one shaky leg to stand on for that claim.

Not all polls are created equal. Like anything else, there are well done ones and poorly done ones. If you combine fourteen high quality national polls held on the eve of the 2016 election, Hillary Clinton's average lead in the popular vote was projected at 1.9 percent. She actually received 2.1 percent more votes than did Donald Trump, but because of the way those votes were distributed among states she only got 227 votes in the Electoral College, that institution created by the Framers to protect us from too much democracy, compared with Trump's 304 votes. The polls were not too far from the actual results. They just bungled the distribution of votes among states.

But ultimately, they got the prediction of who would win wrong. I see at least two reasons why public opinion polls in general appear to be increasingly inaccurate.

One is that fewer people are willing to respond to pollsters than ever before. For whatever reason, either because they don't believe in polling science, or because they feel that polls represent attempts to influence electoral outcomes rather than merely report trends, or because people are increasingly contrary, responses have fallen like dropped anvils in recent years. In the 1970's, response rates to pollsters were over 80 percent, by the 1990's response rates were in still 30 percent or more. Today, response rates regularly fall below 10 percent. This undercuts the random sampling approach unless that tiny fraction of responding voters represents the same opinions as the more than 90 percent who refuse to respond. And one can imagine many reasons that people favoring one candidate versus another might be either more or less likely to respond to a pollster's request.

Second—cover your children's ears and eyes—people will deliberately lie to pollsters no matter how anonymously the poll is conducted. And the more people resent polls, the more they may be likely to lie.

My next-to-favorite example of this fact is from the famous Tucson Garbage Project, where people filled out anonymous questionnaires about their eating and drinking habits. What they didn't know is that researchers would be going through their garbage to check on the accuracy of what they reported. It's not surprising that people had trouble remembering how much meat or fruit juice they consumed, but it shouldn't be so difficult to remember whether or not you had at least one beer during the previous week. Three-quarters of the apparently abstemious citizens of Tucson reported drinking no beer whatsoever during the week. However, only one-quarter of the households had no beer cans or bottles in their garbage. Maybe the others didn't really drink the beer. Maybe they just opened the cans, poured the beer down the drain, and threw away the can.

Right.

My very favorite example inevitably appears whenever and wherever men and women are asked how many heterosexual sex partners they have had in their lives. A little math tells you that the lifetime average number of partners for the two sexes must be the same, since it takes one of each to tango. However men, whether from faulty memory, vanity, or wishful thinking, regularly report about twice as many lifetime sex partners as women. I won't bother to guess which sex has the more accurate memory. I think we all know that.

So if you combine the potential bias from the low response rate with the deliberate lies for whatever reason, it seems to me almost miraculous that our political polls do as well as they do.

On the other hand, nothing challenges scientific investigation like human behavior.

Pride in Your Heritage

M Y great-great-great-great grandfather was known as Tor, the Bear Killer, because he reputedly killed sixty-five bears during his life in the mountains of Norway. I've never felt particularly proud, or ashamed, of grandpa Tor. After all, whatever he accomplished in his life has nothing to do with me. Whatever I have accomplished has nothing to do with him. Some people are proud of their genetic heritage though. Take the organization Daughters of the American Revolution, for instance. To be a member of the DAR as they are commonly known, you have to be a direct female descendant of "a patriot of the American Revolution"— someone who, say, signed the Declaration of Independence or fought (on the colonists' side) in the Revolutionary War. How proud of that distinction should they be though?

What we inherit biologically from our ancestors is DNA. DNA as everyone knows is our genetic material. Your DNA is a unique sequence of about three billion DNA "letters" which make up the book of your ancestry. It's a big book, containing about the same number of letters as you'd find in a thousand King James Bibles.

You inherited half your DNA from your mother, half from your father. This is true for everyone, no exceptions. Your parents inherited half *their* DNA from each of *their* two parents—your grandparents. So one-quarter of your DNA came from each of your four grandparents. Continuing that logic, your four grandparents inherited half of their DNA from each of their two parents, so you inherited one-eighth of your DNA from each of your eight great grandparents, one-sixteenth from each of your sixteen great-great grandparents, and so on, with your number of direct ancestors doubling each generation back through the mists of time.

Go back ten generations, which would be to about the time of the American Revolution, and current members of the DAR each have more than a thousand great-great-great-great-great-great-great-great (let's call them eight-great) grandparents, each of whom gave each DAR member about one-thousandth of the DNA they carry in their bodies today. That doesn't seem like much, but it is still about three million DNA letters from each of those thousand ancestors, which is plenty for scientists to identify. It was enough evidence, for instance, for the DNA of a currently living person to prove beyond a reasonable doubt that Thomas Jefferson fathered at least one child with his slave, Sally Hemmings, something that was widely rumored at the time. If you think about it, a lesson from this expanding pool of ancestors over time is that even if one of your eight-great grandparents was Thomas Jefferson, at least some of your other thousand direct ancestors from that time were statistically likely to be drunks, horse thieves, or worse.

Go back another ten generations, which takes you to about the time that Columbus landed in the New World, and you have over a million eighteen-great grandparents. Back another ten generations from there, to your twenty-eight-great grandparents, we're now in the Middle Ages, and you have more direct ancestors than there were people on earth at the time. At this level, everyone on earth today is pretty much directly descended from some of the same ancestors. I find that a comforting thought.

Our genetic ancestry doesn't stop there, of course. The new fossil hunters, the ones in lab coats brandishing pipettes, who analyze ancient DNA extracted from the bones of people who died thousands of years ago, have discovered that all of our very distant ancestors did not necessarily belong to our own species.

To clarify, DNA extracted from old bones has now revealed that in addition to us, that is modern humans, the only surviving human species, there were at least four and likely even more species of humans roaming the earth forty-five thousand years ago.

One of these species was the Neanderthals. Neanderthals have been known from skeletal remains since the nineteenth century. They had been living in Europe and the Middle East for at least two hundred thousand years before we modern humans arrived. They were stockier than we were. Although they made tools, buried their dead, may have produced exquisite cave art, and certainly had bigger brains than our own direct ancestors, it is generally considered that they were less intelligent. In all likelihood, we drove them to extinction about forty thousand years ago.

The entire DNA sequence of the Neanderthal genome has now been reconstructed. One thing that reconstruction showed is that most of us, those whose ancestors were not confined to sub-Saharan Africa (where Neanderthals never lived), inherited around two percent of our genes from them. Yes, some of our distant ancestors clearly bred with Neanderthals. Neanderthal genes may, in fact, contribute to the diversity of skin and hair color seen throughout Europe and the Middle East today.

Getting back to Tor, the Bear Killer, it turns out now that I've had my own DNA sequenced, that I inherited about as much DNA from him as I did from my nameless Neanderthal ancestors. If I'm going to be proud of Tor, I should probably feel the same about them.

How to Survive a Shark Attack

I NEVER been attacked by a shark, but as a former wild animal trainer I have been attacked by African lions, mountain lions, and one black bear. Moreover, in that former life, I hung out with numerous other wild animal trainers, movie stunt men, and wildlife biologists, who loved nothing more than to tip a glass in the evening and tell war stories of the various animal attacks they have witnessed or survived. Incidentally, the person with the most and best stories, and scars to back the stories up, was not an animal trainer or stuntman but a two-time Emmy-winning wild-life photographer and film maker with an incredible knack for getting the impossible shot and also for getting flipped, ripped, slashed, bashed, and stomped by crocs, rhinos, leopards, hyenas, and chimps.

What's more, I once served on the graduate committee of a student who wrote her Master's thesis on the who-where-what-and-how-bad of more than a thousand documented mountain lions attacks on people. The survival rules for attacks by large predators are unlikely to be all that different if you find yourself in the water or in the woods, so here is what I've learned. It could save your life.

If you really don't want to be attacked by a shark, don't go in the ocean. In 2020, there were thirty-three unprovoked shark attacks in the US, although only three of them were fatal. You may find it comforting to know that only one in eleven shark attacks was deadly, at least in that year. Florida, as usual, had the most attacks, more than three times as many as any other state. Of course, staying on land has its own dangers. Also in 2020, seventeen Americans were killed by lightning and nearly a hundred died in traffic accidents caused by deer. So if you really want to stay safe, don't go in the ocean. If you insist on going in the ocean, don't do it in Florida. Oh, and don't leave your house in the rain or drive a car. Lightning and deer are waiting to get you.

If you insist on swimming or surfing in the ocean, recent research has shown that sharks are most likely to attack in the early morning or late afternoon when the sun is low. They also prefer to attack with the sun behind them, so that the glare on the water makes them difficult to see coming. I take this to mean that the safest time to swim in the ocean on the East Coast is in the late afternoon because for a shark to attack with the sun behind it, it would be coming from the setting sun, which in this case would be from the beach. Since large sharks lounging in beach chairs are fairly conspicuous, you might have plenty of warning. For similar reasons, if you're on the West coast swim in the morning.

Seriously, there are three things that will determine whether you survive an attack by a shark or any other large predator if you are unarmed. First, the size of the predator, second, its purpose in attacking you, and third, your behavior. You control only one of these.

If a very large predator, say a great white shark or grizzly bear, attacks you in full predatory mode, then it makes no difference what you do. You can fight, scream, beg, play dead. It doesn't matter. In the end, you will be dead. A large predator in full attack mode is unlikely to even notice whether you were attempting to fight back versus play dead. On the other hand, if the motive is less clear, then what you do could make a very big difference. In the case of shark attack survivor Mick Fanning, for instance, who was widely credited with fighting off a great white, that shark seemed to be making more of an inquisitive nudge or maybe a nibble rather than an attack. Fanning seemed to understand this as he later thanked the shark for not killing him. In Mick's case, smacking the shark with a fist may have discouraged it from getting even more inquisitive.

You may have heard that it is a good idea to play dead if attacked by a grizzly bear. This is probably good advice as many grizzly bear attacks are defensive, a consequence of someone accidently surprising the bear at close range. As I say, if the bear is intent on killing you, it will. But by playing dead, you might—just might—convince it that you are no threat, and it may smack you around a bit and then go on its way. As you are unlikely to surprise a shark in the open ocean, this advice may not be applicable.

If the predator is smaller, say mountain lion or small shark size, then it also might matter how you react. The Master's student who researched all those mountain lion attacks discovered that many of them were by the mountain lion equivalent of teenagers that were still trying to figure out what size animals they should be attacking. If you fight back in cases like that, giving them more trouble than they expected, they just may run away to hunt another day. In fact, fighting back was by far the most successful strategy against attacking mountain lions. It makes sense. Predators cannot afford to take even small chances of being injured by their prey. Injured animals can't hunt effectively. Predators that can't hunt, starve. No reason to think the same isn't true of sharks.

So the bottom line for surviving shark attacks then is the philosophy Joe Sprinkle made famous. Joe Sprinkle was an oil worker who one day in 1958 stopped to help a seemingly stranded motorist by the side of a Wyoming highway. Little did he know that the man he was trying to help was Charles Starkweather, a man who in the previous eight days had shot, strangled, and stabbed to death ten people, including a two year-old girl as well as the owner of the car he sat in. Just as Joe spotted the owner's body in the car, Starkweather went for his shotgun and Sprinkle went for Starkweather. They were still struggling over the gun minutes later when a police car happened by, at which point Starkweather gave up the fight and fled, to be captured a little while later. When asked whatever possessed him to grapple with a crazed killer like Starkweather, Joe Sprinkle said, "You might as well die fighting." That may be pretty good advice when it comes to sharks too.

Pretty Good Driver, Aren't You

E VEN though I've never met you, I know that you're an above average driver. How do I know? Because one of the quirks of human psychology is that virtually everyone, no matter what their driving history, considers themselves an above average driver.

The classic study revealing this common bit of self-delusion was done more than fifty years ago, but has been repeated many times since. In that study, researchers Caroline Preston and Stanley Harris interviewed fifty people who were currently hospitalized from traffic accidents in which they were the driver. Most of these accidents were described as "hit fixed object" hard enough to overturn the car. Police reports placed clear blame on the hospitalized drivers in more than two-thirds of these accidents and suggested it in most of the others. Yet when asked to rate their driving skills, the hospitalized drivers rated themselves closer to "expert" than to "very poor" on a nine point scale. A second group of drivers, matched to the accident group in terms of age, sex, race, and education level, all with excellent driving records rated themselves exactly the same as the hospitalized accident group.

I'm sorry, folks. We may all *think* we're above average, but we can't all actually *be* above average. An average by definition is a middle value. There should be roughly the same number below average as above average. Since it's obviously not us, it must be those *other* people who are deluding themselves about their driving skills.

So let's all agree that *you and I* are above average, but what about other people similar to us? What determines how well they drive? On this, there are statistics galore, so we might be able to figure out the people, or rather the groups, who really are good drivers from those *other* people, the ones that are accidents waiting to happen.

Let's take age as one indicator. Here figuring it out is pretty easy. Automobile insurance companies have done all the leg work and as you can tell from insurance rates, teenagers are terrible drivers. In the vast majority of states, the minimum age for unsupervised driving is sixteen. In that first year of eligibility, teenagers don't drive all that much, which it turns out is a good thing. Their accident rate *per mile driven* is about twice as high as any other age group, six times as high as the safest driving age group who are those—wait for it—in their sixties. Of course teenage boys generally suffer temporary insanity lasting only a decade or two due to surging testosterone, so it is not surprising that they account for two-thirds of teenage accidents. Even drivers over age eighty, poor eyes, poor hearing, bad reflexes and all, have only about one-third the accident rate of sixteen-year-olds.

Does where you live affect how good a driver you are? You betcha, as they might say in Minnesota, which is tied for lowest traffic accident death rate among the fifty states. The other safest driving states are Massachusetts, a shocker to those of us who have survived driving in Boston, and Rhode Island.

Some of the drivers with the worst reputations, I'm looking at you California and New York, actually have pretty low death rates from car crashes. The worst drivers, as measured by deaths per mile driven, are in the southeastern states. South Carolina tops the list, followed by Kentucky, Mississippi, Louisiana, and Arkansas with Alabama not far behind. The outlier among bad driving states is Alaska, by far the biggest state with by far the fewest cars, but still with a traffic fatality rate right up there with the big boys down South. I'm wondering who else is around for Alaskans to collide with? Moose? Grizzlies?

Given that we are all confident that we are above average drivers, does our degree of self-confidence affect how good a driver we actually are? As I say, overestimation of driving ability is a common human trait, but some people overestimate themselves more than others.

An interesting study compared American and Swedish drivers. Both groups were asked to rate their driving skill and driving safety qualities relative to other drivers. The Swedes, like everyone else, overestimated themselves. More than three-fourths of Swedes rated themselves above average on driving safety and about two-thirds rated themselves above average in skill. In terms of overconfidence though, Americans left them in the dust. Nearly 90 percent of Americans rated themselves above average in safe driving and a whopping 93 percent rated themselves above average in skill.

What's wrong with overconfidence, I can hear you saying. Overconfidence made us think we could put a man on the moon in less than a decade, and maybe helped us actually do it. That may be true, but overconfidence also gave us General Custer, the Titanic, and the 1929 stock market crash.

How is that overconfidence working out for driving? Not so well, it turns out, more like Custer than the moonshot. The somewhat overconfident Swedish have less than half the traffic fatality rate as the very overconfident Americans.

It's nice that we all think can so well of ourselves. You know who else thinks so well of us? Tow truck drivers and wrecking yard owners.

Is Technology Making Us Stupid?

NOT long ago, I bought a small item at my local market. I forget what it was, but I remember that it cost $1.67 because of what followed. When the cashier saw me reach for cash, she assumed that I would hand her two dollars. In fact, she was so sure that she punched that amount into the cash register. When the cash drawer popped open and I handed her a five dollar bill instead, she suddenly looked very worried. It took me a while to realize, as I watched her fidget and stare at the register, that her worry had to do with figuring out how much change I was owed.

Cash registers were invented in the late nineteenth century to prevent employee theft. For most of their history, they were nothing more than fancy adding machines, keeping track of the total of each sale and also of all sales together. Cashiers had to punch in the price of each item. The register kept a running total and when all items were totaled, it displayed the total amount of your purchase. The cash drawer popped open, the cashier took your money, and counted out your change. At the end of each day, cash registers allowed store owners to know how much money should be in the till. If there was less than this amount, the cashier had some explaining to do.

Modern, computerized, cash registers require no knowledge of arithmetic, not even the simple third grade arithmetic necessary to count out change. Cashiers no longer punch in the price of items. They either scan them in or punch a button with the name of the item on it. The register still presents the total though. If some Luddite like myself insists on paying with actual money instead of a card, the cashier punches in the amount you hand her (or him), and the register spits out the amount of change owed. The chance for human error is reduced. Checkout lines move faster.

But human error is not eliminated. In my case, the cashier had punched in the wrong amount and now had to figure out the correct change on her own. She was flying solo with no parachute.

Well not quite solo. Eventually, she reached for her smart phone. She couldn't figure out the correct change using the calculator on her phone either. By now, the people in line behind me were growing restive. I had been trying to help for some time. "That would be three dollars and thirty-three cents," I repeated for about the fifth time. "Just add three dollars to what the register says," Clearly, I was trying to pull some kind of scam. She continued to ignore me.

The manager finally noticed one increasingly long line of irritated customers and came over to see what the problem was. He tried, without luck, to figure it out on her smart phone too. Finally, to avoid a riot by exasperated customers, they somewhat belligerently asked me "three dollars, thirty-three cents?" Yes, I said. Riot averted.

Now, I'm sure this is an exceptional case. The overwhelming majority of cashiers and store managers could no doubt do this arithmetic on their own if they had to. In fact, I'm sure these two could have done it when they graduated from third grade because they would have been practicing it then. The point is that if we quit using a skill because a machine has taken it over, we will eventually lose that skill, even if it may be important for other aspects of life.

My cashier and store manager had become innumerate, a word coined by author Douglas Hofstadter, meaning incapable of being comfortable with understanding and manipulating simple numbers. Innumeracy of some degree has always been with us, but I think that because of the availability of calculators it is much worse than ever before. Calculators are enormously useful as well as convenient for many things. But we now use them for simple calculations we used to do in our heads. One consequence of this is that we lose our feel for simple numbers and simple numbers connect us to the real world.

Simple numbers, for instance, tell us about actual risks. We can all understand what the weather man means when he says that there is a 50 percent chance of rain tomorrow. However, if the weatherman says that there is a 50 percent chance of rain on Saturday and a 50 percent chance on Sunday, a depressing number of people interpret that to mean that there is a 100 percent chance of rain over the weekend. If you can't understand why that answer is wrong, your smart phone will not help you.

The same lack of comfort with simple numbers can mislead us in life decisions. As John Allen Paulos, a mathematician who published the bestselling book *Innumeracy* in 1988, has pointed out, innumeracy is often behind the gap between how scientists (who are forced by their profession to be numerate) and the rest of the public perceive risk. For instance, Americans in general are vastly more worried about terrorist attacks, particularly those by immigrant Jihadi terrorists, than the numbers indicate they should be. In fact, the average annual number of Americans killed in such attacks is about thirty-five times less than the number killed by lawnmowers. Yet our politics can be dominated by worries about terrorist attacks not lawnmower attacks.

Innumeracy also misleads us about the relationships among large numbers. You know the attitude—millions, billions, trillions, whatever. And that can mislead us about many other things. For instance, Americans hear that the government spends over thirty-five billion dollars on foreign aid and assume that that is way too much. It may well be too much, but in fact it is less than 1 percent of the federal budget. A Kaiser Family Foundation poll found that the average American thought it was 26 percent of the Federal budget.

I could go on and on but instead I'll just suggest that everyone read the book *Innumeracy*, which is more relevant than ever more than thirty years after it was first published. And while you are doing so, put down the calculator for simple things. Your mathematical brain could use to exercise too.

Who Starts the Rain?

I F your self-confidence is still recovering from the discovery than you are in fact a minority occupant of your own body, I have some good news for you. I'm referring, of course, to the often quoted figure that the total number of bacterial cells in and on your body outnumbers what you think of as your own cells by a ten to one margin.

That turns out to have been an exaggeration.

You're still outnumbered, just not that bad. The ten to one figure came from a back-of-the-table-napkin guestimate made more than forty years ago and never scientifically validated. Forty years ago, we didn't know squat about bacteria compared to today. More sophisticated calculations by a team of Israeli scientists recently determined that there are really only about 25 percent more bacterial cells in and on you than the number of your own cells.

That's the good news.

The bad news is that if you add up all of the genes in all of those bacteria, you turn out to own less than 1 percent of all the genes in your own body.

Even worse news is how much of our lives those bacteria and all their genes control. Modern microbiologists think that the bacteria inside our intestines where the vast majority of them live, do much more than just help us digest our food or give us an occasional bout of diarrhea as we used to think. Many researchers now think that our intestinal bacteria can make us crave particular foods, food that they—the bacteria—need, not necessarily foods that we need. They have also been hypothesized to be able to make us more or less hungry, therefore more or less obese. Also, intestinal bacteria are now being blamed, maybe unfairly but maybe not, for problems ranging from mood swings to anxiety, depression, even autism and Alzheimer's disease.

That's not all. Bacterial societies living on our skin can give our skin that healthy glow or if we're less fortunate give us acne, psoriasis, dandruff, a host of autoimmune diseases, and even make us more (or less) attractive to mosquitoes.

And the bacteria living in our mouths, estimated to be about seven hundred different species, can protect our teeth from decay and our gums from infection, but depending on the species mixture can also give us swollen diseased gums, bad breath, pneumonia, or even heart problems.

If all that weren't spooky enough, now it appears that bacteria may control our weather too.

I know that sounds crazy, but hear me out.

Clouds as everyone knows are formed from droplets of water too tiny to fall to the ground. One of the persistent mysteries of weather is why some clouds produce rain or snow while others with just as much water in them produce nothing but a threatening sky. It turns out this has mostly to do with the intricacies of ice formation inside the clouds.

Most rain begins as ice, because ice crystals once they begin forming inside clouds, grow rapidly until they are big enough to plummet to the ground. Most often the ice melts as it falls, so by the time it hits your umbrella, it is water again.

Almost all clouds are at altitudes where the air temperature is colder than what you were taught was the freezing point of water, zero degrees Celsius or thirty-two degrees Fahrenheit. What you were taught wasn't wrong exactly. It was incomplete though. Pure water such as found in clouds can remain liquid to as cold as forty degrees below zero its traditional freezing point in a process called super-cooling. What water in clouds needs to begin coalescing into ice is a solid surface on which water molecules can organize themselves to form ice.

Until recently, most meteorologists assumed that this organizing surface was dust or soot particles blown up from the ground. Often that may be the case. But it is increasingly looking like some bacteria are specialists at turning cloud water into ice and that ice into rain.

The first person to make this connection was David Sands, a Montana-based plant biologist, who forty years ago was puzzled because he just couldn't figure out why he couldn't get rid of a bacterial disease that was attacking his wheat. He suspected that particles as small as bacteria should be as easily whisked into the sky as could dust or soot, and if so, it might be carried back to land on his wheat again when it rained. To test this idea, he rented a plane, flew through some clouds, and collected from inside the clouds exactly the bacteria that caused his wheat disease just as he had suspected.

What he didn't suspect at the time, but what we now know, is that the bacterium in question, called *Pseudomonas syringae*, as well as many other bacteria species, had genes that seem to be specialized for the sole purpose of producing proteins that turn super-cooled water droplets into ice. They are much more effective at this, in fact, than dust or soot.

Sand's discovery of bacteria in clouds inspired other researchers to look at clouds in more detail. Now we know of hundreds of bacteria species that spend part of their time in clouds. Some of these are found as high as seven miles in the air. More impressively, bacteria with genes that manufacture ice-nucleating proteins have been found in rain drops, in fresh snow, even in hail stones so huge they were preserved for posterity in museums. Skiers should be thankful for this discovery, because now machines that make artificial snow use some of these same bacteria to help produce a better quality snow substitute.

Consider this scenario now from a bacterium's point of view. You are able make the rain to nourish the plants that provide you with your home and your food. Yes, I forgot to mention that these bacteria cause plant diseases precisely because they dine on nutrients released from damaged plant cells. In fact, ice-nucleating proteins may have evolved not to cause it to rain, but to help form ice crystals, which can break open plant cells. Rainmaking may have been just a surprise bonus.

Okay, I exaggerated a bit. Bacteria don't really control all the weather. They can't make it rain where there is no moisture in the air. They can't control the wind strength or direction. But it looks like they just might be responsible for some of those showers that help relieve drought. So next time it rains, you might give a quiet "thank you" to the bacteria in your garden.

IX.

Evolving Science

Darwin in the Twenty-First Century

I n one of those historical coincidences that makes you question the indifference of the universe, the greatest statesman and greatest scientist of the nineteenth century were born on the same day of the same year, just hours, and an ocean, apart. Yes, Abraham Lincoln and Charles Darwin were both born on February 12, 1809. Despite their very different beginnings—Lincoln, son of a farmer, famously born in a one-room log cabin and Darwin, son of an eminent physician, born into a family of wealthy intellectuals—they had a surprising amount in common in addition to their lasting fame. Both lost their mothers to illness when they were still children. Both were devastated by the loss of several of their own young children. Both were prone to gloom and depression later in life. And both abominated slavery.

Lincoln without doubt had the greater immediate legacy, having preserved the United States as a single country and officially abolished slavery throughout it. But today he is largely a revered figure of the past.

Darwin, on the other hand, is very much a figure of the present. His discovery of the principle of natural selection continues to provide us with insights—and cautionary tales—about modern life. At present, we are suffering through the worst pandemic in more than a century, approaching nearly six million dead globally, which is the result of a newly evolved, continually evolving, highly successful virus. Let's consider the many less obvious ways in which Darwin's discovery and modern life intertwine.

Darwinian algorithms, random change followed by selection of the best of the random variants, are now used by pharmaceutical companies in the design of new drugs, by computer scientists to improve the quality and speed of problem-solving programs, and of course by amateur brewers and marijuana farmers to improve the quality of their products. Recent books employ the selection principle to describe *Darwinian Medicine*, *Darwinian Agriculture*, *Darwinian Economics*, even *Darwinian Detectives* seeking to understand how our genome evolved.

Evolutionary principles also help us understand ecosystem level events, such as why more and more insects are less and less affected by our pesticides, and what the consequences will be for the rest of the ecosystem. They also give us insight into smaller scale, but critical, events such as how we can *prevent* cancer and HIV, not to mention SARS-CoV-2, from becoming increasingly resistant to therapeutic drugs over time.

In all these specialized fields, evolutionary tools—thanks to Darwin's discovery—are in daily use. Unfortunately, this message, like the message of much of science, hasn't penetrated so well to the public at large, as the refusal to be vaccinated against COVID-19 shows. This can also be seen in the way we slosh antibiotics carelessly about in our environment. About 80 percent of all antibiotics are not used for medical purposes at all, but are given to livestock to increase their growth rate. Antibiotics are also sprayed on fruit orchards to prevent blemishes and blight.

The consequence in a world awash in antibiotics is that antibiotic-resistant bacteria have a survival advantage over susceptible bacteria and quickly predominate, making antibiotics ineffective when they are needed to fight potentially deadly infections. Antibiotic-resistant bacteria are now everywhere. Recently, they've even been found in seawater and penguin colonies in Antarctica.

Antibiotics only became widely available after World War II and since then have saved millions of lives, including mine, more than once. However, antibiotics more and more often fail to help those who need them. In fact, more people died last year from antibiotic-resistance bacteria than by HIV or malaria. These same germs that were easily killed by antibiotics a decade ago are now immune to even our most powerful drugs.

Doctors, who should know better, and patients, if they've ever been exposed to evolutionary reasoning as they should have been in school, should know better too. Yet a recent study found that nine of ten doctors reported caving in to the wishes of demanding patients who wanted antibiotic prescriptions even though they didn't need them. A surprising 97 percent of patients who ask for antibiotic prescriptions get them, whether they need them or not.

Hospitals are particularly dangerous places now, because widespread antibiotic use cannot be avoided there. As a result, the worst bugs, sometimes resistant to every known antibiotic, lurk in hospitals. Ironically, evolutionary principles tell us how to slow, and possibly prevent or reverse, the steady march of antibiotic resistance, even in hospitals. However, it requires the will, the foresight, and the knowledge to implement appropriate solutions.

Darwinian logic can still save us, but Darwinian principles, if ignored, could also do us in. As I said, Charles Darwin is very much a figure of the present.

Darwin's Foresight

CHARLES Darwin envied Jemmy Button's eyesight.

You would too.

Acute vision was important at sea in 1831 when twenty-two year old Darwin and fourteen year old Jemmy Button found themselves together aboard a sailing ship, *The Beagle*, which was surveying the coast of South America. Acute vision could spot the tiny dot of a ship or a storm on the horizon. Was it coming this way? Was it a pirate ship or friendly?

Actually young Charles was vain about his own eyesight. Although it was generally agreed that sailors, after years of practice at sea, could see things on the horizon that landlubbers would never spot, Darwin could see farther than practically any of the sailors. But Jemmy was in another realm. He could *identify* distant objects that no one else could even see.

It wasn't just Jemmy. The other two native South Americans on board, York Minster and Fuegia Basket, could see just as well. All three came from hunter-gatherer tribes that eked out a living on the rocky, rain- and wind-swept coast of Tierra del Fuego at the southern tip of South America.

Darwin didn't appreciate it at the time, but he was experiencing an example of the great principle he discovered a few years later, the principle of natural selection. For generations the quality of one's vision had scarcely mattered to Darwin's country gentleman ancestors. But for Jemmy, York, and Fuegia, whose ancestors had been living in a particularly unforgiving environment on the edge of starvation for centuries, being able to spot from a distance the seal or the otter or the seabird they hunted was a matter of survival. Weak vision was a death sentence. And as the joke goes, if your parents didn't survive long enough to have kids, chances are that you won't either.

Darwin's memories of Jemmy Button's remarkable eyesight may have been why he used the example of the "perfect and complex" eye to describe how natural selection could mold such perfection by degrees. Maybe it's because my eyesight has never been especially good, maybe it's something else, but I'm not so impressed by the human eye. Compared to what they might be, our eyes seem pretty pathetic to me.

For instance, light is all around us yet we can't see it. What we call "light" that we do see is just a thin sliver of the radiant energy that fills our universe. Radio waves, microwaves, infrared, ultraviolent, x-rays. It's all the same kind of so-called electromagnetic radiation, but carries vastly different amounts of energy. It travels in waves like ripples on a pond at, well, the speed of light. Some of the energy wavelengths, the distance between the ripples, as it were, excite pigments in our eyes so we can see them. Others don't.

If your visual pigments happened to be excited by microwaves, you could watch the light show inside the box where your food is cooking. Actually, the moisture inside the food in that box *is* excited by microwaves. So excited that it heats up, cooking your food in the process.

If those pigments could be excited by radio waves you could watch the music and the nonsense pouring out of radio towers.

If your visual pigments happened to be excited by infrared, you could see your television remote flashing at your television.

Actually some animals like rattlesnakes do have pigments that are excited by infrared. Rattlesnakes have daytime vision like we do, but they also have an extra set of eyes called pit organs that are specialized for seeing warm bodies in the dark. They see the infrared they we radiate. Devious researches discovered this by noticing that rattlesnakes could accurately strike warm objects such as mice or rats even in absolute darkness. Rattlesnakes don't see cold-blooded animals like frogs or lizards in the dark. But they do see you.

If you could see ultraviolet light, you might see flowers like a honeybee does. Many flowers have ultraviolet "nectar guides," bull's-eyes of ultraviolet-reflecting pigments highlighting where the nectar can be found. You might also be able to see trails of rodent urine in the, because rodent urine also reflects ultraviolet light. Some birds of prey are thought to track prey this way.

If you could see x-rays, well, that wouldn't be all that useful, because energy at the wavelength of x-rays passes right through many things that you might want to see and avoid. X-ray vision despite what superman might say, would have you bumping into a lot of things that you wouldn't know were there.

When I say that we see only a thin sliver of radiation, I'm not kidding. We only see about one octave among the thousands of octaves of light.

What do I mean by that?

Sound is a different kind of energy, but it comes in wavelengths too. Long wavelengths make low-pitch sounds, short wavelengths maker high-pitch sounds. A doubling of the wavelength of a sound lowers it by an octave on a musical instrument. The eighty-eight keys of a piano cover a little more than seven octaves. Humans can hear a broader range notes than a piano has. We hear about ten octaves. At least we can hear ten octaves when we're ten years old, the age our hearing is most sensitive. Peak hearing sensitivity may be even younger now that so many ten year olds seem to have permanently implanted ear buds injuring their ears earlier in life.

Getting back to the miserable little sliver of light we can actually see, the wavelength of red light, the longest wavelength we can see is only twice the wavelength of violet, the shortest we can see. One visual octave. One-tenth the range of sounds we can hear. As I say, pathetic.

We also can't see anything much smaller than a grain of sand. Most of the life on earth, the entire microbial world, is smaller than a grain of sand. Without microscopes we wouldn't know it exists.

We can't see things that move too fast either. Like bullets or even ball bearings shot from a slingshot. Flies see rapid movement much better than we do. Compared to us, they see the world in slow motion, which is why it's so hard to swat them.

Maybe I'm a glass-half-full person. Darwin certainly was not. We should remember that he found, as he so elegantly put it, a "grandeur in this view of life." All around him, he saw "forms most beautiful and most wonderful." Of course, he had very good eyesight.

It's in Your DNA

O N February 28, 1953 two brash young men strode into *The Eagle* pub in Cambridge, England and loudly announced to anyone within earshot that they had just discovered the secret of life. James Watson and Francis Crick had, indeed, just discovered the chemical structure of DNA. For once in their lives though, Watson and Crick may have been overly modest. They had discovered much more than the mere secret of life.

DNA, as everyone knows by now, is a double helix. That is, it resembles a long twisted rope ladder in which every rung is made up of two of the four DNA "letters" joined together. The order of these rung-letters along the ladder is unique to every individual (except for identical twins) and every species. Your DNA determines whether you are a pea plant, a peacock, or a person, not to mention also determining what sort of pea plant, peacock, or person you are.

But beyond its role in inheritance, DNA turned out to be astonishing in many other ways. For starters, that DNA ladder turned out to be very, very long. The human genome, for instance, is about three billion DNA letters long. That's a lot of coded information. In fact, there are as many DNA letters in each of your cells as there are in a thousand copies of the King James Bible. On the other hand, the marbled lungfish, no doubt your favorite fish, has more than forty times that length of DNA it each of its cells.

The total length of DNA inside your body almost defies reason. If you straightened out and lined up the DNA ladder in one of cells of your body, it would be about one yard in length. The precise twisting, coiling, and recoiling required to pack that amount of DNA inside something as small as a human cell is itself pretty remarkable. A colleague of mine once described it as like stuffing fifty miles of fishing line into a blueberry.

Even more remarkably, if you straightened out and lined up all the DNA from all the roughly forty trillion cells in your body, it would stretch from earth to the demoted planet Pluto in the outer reaches of our solar system and back again ten times. Also, because you are continually shedding cells from your body, from your skin and from the lining of all thousands of miles of tubes and tunnels inside you, in order to replace those cells, your body must manufacture about two thousand miles of new DNA every second of every day of your life! No wonder you're bushed come Friday.

Once we discovered how to determine the exact sequence of any DNA strand, it allowed us to unambiguously identify the species or individual from which that DNA came. Suddenly, DNA flooded every aspect of our lives. It became the ultimate truth detector. Yes, you are (or are not) the father of that child. Yes, you were (or were not) present at that crime scene. Yes, that bottle of herbal supplement does (or surprisingly often, does not) contain the ingredients it says on the label. No, that fish you bought at the supermarket is (or sometimes is not) the species the market claims it is.

Yes, Thomas Jefferson did father children by his slave Sally Hemmings. No, the Russian princess Anastasia did not survive the massacre of the rest of her family by Bolsheviks in 1918 and go on to live out her life in San Francisco. Yes, the skeleton discovered under that parking lot was that of the evil King Richard III, who died at the Battle of Bosworth Field in 1485.

DNA allowed us to discover a previously invisible new world of microbial life. Prior to the use of DNA sequencing to identify microbial species, we knew very little about microbes other than those few we could grow in a laboratory dish, in a laboratory animal, or in a human host. It turns out that was probably less than 1 percent of all the microbes out there.

Now, thanks to our constantly increasing ability to sequence long stretches of DNA, we have identified thousands upon thousands of new microbial species. Hundreds to thousands of newly described species live just inside your digestive tract, for instance, and affect your health in many ways. We found that microbes coat practically everything and live practically everywhere, on and even in, the earth. Newly discovered microbes were found in boiling hot springs, in Antarctic lakes buried under a half mile of ice for millions of years, in the deepest parts of the ocean, even inside rocks. Microbes detected only by their DNA are found in the hottest, coldest, driest, darkest, saltiest, and most radioactive places on earth.

Unfortunately, that's about all we know about them, their DNA sequence and where they live.

By the way, progress in increasing the speed, and lowering the cost, of DNA sequencing has been almost as remarkable as the discovery of this new microbial world. The first complete sequence of a human genome, fittingly enough, James Watson's genome, took thirteen years and cost three billion dollars. Now, a little more than two decades later, a human genome can be sequenced in a few hours and costs less than a dinner for two at a fine restaurant. Soon your genome sequence will be a standard item in your medical records.

In addition to the bonanza of new microbes, DNA has led to the discovery of new species that were right in front of our eyes. Two populations of giant tortoises living only twelve miles apart on Santa Cruz Island in the Galápagos Islands were recently discovered to actually be two separate species. What used to be one species of giraffe is now four. What used to be one orangutan species is now three, and you will be happy to learn that the world of spotted skunks now consists of seven species rather than four.

DNA floating free in the environment allows us to detect the presence of rare and hard to find species. Recently the elusive, two-foot long salamander, appropriately named the hellbender, was discovered to exist in a number of streams here in the southeastern United States, not from physical sightings but from DNA recovered from stream water.

Because the DNA sequence of closely-related species (or individuals) is more similar than more distantly-related species (or individuals), DNA has allowed us to fill in the details in the tree of life that fossils were inadequate to tell us. It revealed, for instance, that we are closer evolutionary relatives of mice than we are of dogs. We have learned that the most common and devastating form of HIV jumped from chimpanzees to humans in southeastern Cameroon in the early twentieth century and that sometime before that it jumped to chimpanzees from the small monkeys chimpanzees occasionally eat.

Watson and Crick could never have suspected how long DNA can survive outside a living body. The oldest identifiable ancient DNA discovered so far came from the molar tooth from a mammoth that died and was preserved in the Siberian permafrost a little more than one million years ago. Sorry *Jurassic Park* fans, that's less than 2 percent of the distance back to the extinction of the last dinosaur. But there is now a serious effort to genetically revive the woolly mammoth by inserting some of its DNA into the genome of its closet living relative, the Asian elephant.

So were those giddily confident young men shouting that they had discovered the secret of life in a Cambridge pub in 1953 underplaying their discovery? You be the judge.

Dolly's Twenty-Fifth Birthday

W HO had three mothers, no father, an identical twin, and was named after a country music star?

No, this isn't a quiz about characters from a *Star Trek* movie. If you guessed Dolly, the sheep, give yourself a pat on the back.

Dolly, the first cloned mammal, burst into public view some twenty-five years ago as of this October 2021 writing. For those of you who don't remember, Dolly created an international sensation. Many scientists—and nearly everyone else—up to that time thought that cloning mammals was close to impossible.

The implications of reproduction-by-cloning had bioethicists chewing on their pillows. Were we now facing a brave new world where armies of identical babies could be mass produced? Who would be the parents of those mass produced babies? Were wealthy narcissists about to populate the world with carbon copies of themselves? Would they create babies just to provide themselves with replacement organs when they grew old and their own organs began to fail?

With a quarter of a century of perspective and experience, it might be time to consider what Dolly has—and has not—wrought.

First, let's sort out the three mothers. Dolly was cloned from a mammary gland cell of a six-year-old ewe, mother number one. Mammary gland is biology-speak for the body part that Dolly Parton has a famous pair of, which is why her scientific creators gave her, the sheep, that name. Dolly, the singer, accepted this tribute gracefully, noting that there is no such thing as baaaaaaad publicity.

The mammary cell from mother number one was fused with mother number two's unfertilized egg from which the genetic material was removed. The resulting embryo was implanted in, and carried to term by, mother number three.

Dolly was an almost exact genetic copy of mother number one. I'll explain the "almost" shortly.

Notice that no males were involved in this new method of reproducing. As my wife said at the time, "well, there goes the last thing that men are good for." A friend predicted that in a hundred years, the entire human population would be descended from a dozen female medical students from the early twenty-first century.

However twenty-five years later with several dozen other species having been cloned this way, men are no longer feeling quite so threatened. Despite several unproven claims by publicity seekers, no cloned human babies have been produced. People, it seems, prefer to make babies the old-fashioned way. However, the barrier to making cloned babies is now mainly ethical and regulatory rather than technical. Eventually, someone with enough money, enough power, and enough narcissism will do it. Get ready.

Where reproductive cloning, as it is called, *has* taken off is in livestock and sport. Cattle that are elite meat or milk producers are now routinely cloned. Although it is banned in Europe, in America most of us have probably eaten or drunk the products of cloned cows. China is planning to produce a hundred thousand cloned cattle per year and is expected to expand the operation to one million cattle per year, as quickly as possible. More than seven hundred horses have been cloned so far and it won't be long before they are running and jumping in Olympic equestrian events. In fact, a team of six horses, all cloned from the same former champion, has already helped Argentinian polo player, Adolfo Cambiaso, win a high-profile match in Buenos Aires.

Cloning, even today, is not cheap. It is still technically demanding and many embryos need to be produced for every one that makes it to adulthood. A cloned horse, for instance, will set you back eighty-five thousand dollars at today's prices. On the other hand, if that cloned horse is Secretariat, it might be worth it. It might be worth it, but it wouldn't be legal. Thoroughbred racing, at least in the United States, excludes all horses that weren't produced by the traditional union of one stallion with one mare, or a "live cover" as the horsey euphemism goes. We like our racing horses to make babies the old fashioned way too.

Narcissism, of course, is not the only motivation for reproductive cloning. Grief can be a very real motivator as well. Wouldn't it be nice to be able to re-create a favorite pet that had died?

If you have the money, in fact, there are commercial services that will do just that. At today's prices, a cloned dog costs around fifty grand, a cat is half of that. Cat lovers, before you contact me, I'm told that this price difference is no reflection on the relative worth of dogs versus cats. Cats just happen to be easier to clone. If you're not sure whether or not you want to go through with cloning Spike, your favorite dog, services are also offered to freeze and preserve some of Spike's cells for a fraction of the cost. This gives you the option of deciding later on if you really want to wake up the cells and turn them into Spike II.

Yes, this is possible but you should realize that you aren't really re-creating your pet.

Remember I said that Dolly was an almost exact genetic copy of mother number one, whose udder cell donated her genetic material? *Almost* is a key word.

Dolly had all genes from the nucleus of mother number one's cell, but she also had another genome as we all do.

Inside your cells are tiny sausage-like objects called mitochondria that produce most of your cells' energy. They have their own genome. It is small, only thirteen protein-making genes, compared to around twenty thousand genes in the nucleus. However, because those genes are crucial for providing energy, these thirteen genes are particularly important. Small mutations in them cause everything from exercise intolerance to muscle wasting and epilepsy to blindness and deafness. Whereas you have only two copies of the genes in each cell's nucleus, you have anywhere from a few thousand to as many as a hundred thousand copies of the mitochondrial genes in each of your cells. Dolly's mitochondrial genes were all from the unfertilized egg, mother number two. Mitochondrial genes in traditional reproduction as well as in reproductive cloning are inherited only from the egg. Only mothers can pass down mitochondria to offspring. Men, here is something else we can't do ourselves.

To show how important this can be, recent research has shown that mice with identical nuclear genes, but with different mitochondrial genes, can be fat or thin, energetic or lethargic, more or less susceptible to heart problems, shorter-lived or longer-lived.

So, if you really want to clone a horse that can run like Secretariat, you need not only his cells, you need an unfertilized egg from his mother or from one of her female descendants, because a lot of his running ability may have come from his mother's mitochondrial genes.

Spike II is likely to differ from the original Spike in many ways, regardless of how identical they may look, because they will have different mitochondrial genes. Of course, they will have also been raised in different environments. Even the environment of the uterus within which a fetus develops turns out to be surprisingly important to later life, health, and personality.

Dolly has already had a bigger impact on livestock than I expected. She may yet do so in the horsey world and among well-to-do pet owners too. However, by far her biggest contribution is something that I haven't mentioned yet.

Let's take that up next.

Dolly's Other Contribution
Making Babies from Scratch

F OR those of us inclined to worry, the creation of Dolly the sheep more than twenty-five years ago signaled that males were expendable. Dolly, you may recall, was a cloned copy of her long-dead mother. Dolly was made by thawing a frozen skin cell from the mammary gland of her mother, merging it with a fresh sheep's egg from which the genetic material had been removed, then implanting it in the uterus of a living ewe where she developed to term. No sperm—no male, that is—was involved. Today, that piece of reproductive technology seems almost quaint. Now, not only do males seem expendable, females, at least living females could one day be expendable too.

The first significant artificial reproductive technology used in people was IVF, *in vitro* fertilization, itself now more than forty-five years old. IVF consists of combining eggs and sperm in a laboratory dish, allowing the resulting embryos to begin developing and then implanting a few of them in a woman's uterus where one or more may develop to term. IVF solved a variety of human fertility problems. There were a number of ethical concerns about IVF raised at the time, but familiarity breeds acceptance. Today IVF has become commonplace and the ethical concerns have faded. Nearly 2 percent of babies in western Europe and the United States are now produced by IVF.

Dolly showed that sperm could be eliminated from this reproductive mix. You still need fresh sheep eggs and the uteruses of living ewes to make new sheep though. Dolly's more subtle, and no doubt more important, message was that skin cells, or cells from other organs for that matter, contain all the genetic information required to make a whole new individual. Therefore, it must contain also the information to make all two hundred or so other cell types that a body contains, brain cells, liver cells, heart cells, and so on. In principle that means that if someone has defective brain or heart cells, we ought to be able to replace those defective cells with newly-created healthy cells from the person's own skin. For instance, diabetic children might be given new insulin-making cells. Stroke or Alzheimer's disease sufferers might get replacement brain cells.

Pursuing that vision, Japanese scientist Shinya Yamanaka in 2006 reported that he had done exactly that, discovered how to reprogram skin cells into stem cells which have the potential to be transformed into any other type of cell. For that accomplishment, he was awarded a Nobel Prize just six years later.

One problem though. There was a lot of guesswork in the procedures required to transform these skin-derived stem cells into other specific cell types. You might end up with brain or heart cells when you were trying to make liver cells. More commonly, you might end up with a mixture of cell types or even cells that resembled, but weren't quite identical, to the cells you were trying to make.

Over time though, researchers have begun to figure out the experimental tricks needed to transform these skin-derived stem cells into exactly the cell type of choice. By 2016, they had even discovered how to make both eggs and sperm from skin cells—in mice, anyway. This means that at least for mice, being an actual living being is no longer a requirement for continuing to make babies. A few mouse skin cells sitting in the freezer plus the womb of a live mouse is all you need to make more mice. Researchers have not yet quite replicated this process using human cells, but they are getting there.

In the last few years, researchers have done something potentially more earthshaking. Several years back, scientists at Cambridge University in the United Kingdom mixed together several types of human stem cells, the cells, remember, that can make all other cell types, and without any eggs or sperm these stem cells within a few days had assembled themselves into something that looked very much like a two week-old human embryo. At that stage of development, an embryo is too advanced to be implanted in a human uterus, but these "embryoids," as they have been called, could potentially grow into viable babies if we developed good enough artificial wombs (and if they were as similar to normal human embryos as they appeared).

Let me emphasize that the aim of experiments like these is not to discover how to mass-produce designer babies in row after row of artificial wombs as in Aldous Huxley's novel *Brave New World*. Scientists pursue this line of research in order to gain a better understanding of very early events in human development, something that might eventually lead to better prevention of birth defects.

Still, the possibility is there. In fact, researchers interested in the end of pregnancy rather than its beginning *are* trying to develop artificial wombs. They are doing so with the goal of increasing the survival in prematurely-born babies. At present, babies born at 23-24 weeks gestation have less than a 50 percent chance of survival and those born even more prematurely have virtually no chance of surviving. Artificial wombs might change these odds. Some promising research on artificial wombs using lambs has recently been reported.

So working from both ends of pregnancy it is conceivable that in the future no actual humans need be involved in making babies. Laboratory robots could in theory unfreeze skin cells from long dead people, transform them into stem cells by well-established methods, assemble those cells into embryos, which could then be grown into living babies in manufactured wombs. No scientists to my knowledge have any ambition to do such a thing, but given the so-called artificial intelligence we are increasingly programming into our robots, who knosws what they might decide to do if they had the power to make an endless supply of human babies from scratch?

For those of us inclined to worry, these possibilities seem a lot more worrisome than simply making males expendable.

Race, It's Only Skin Deep

T HE village of Cheddar in southwest England began producing its famous cheese at least nine hundred years ago. Caves near the village provided the ideal temperature and humidity for maturing that uniquely-flavored dairy product. The caves, it turns out, also provided ideal conditions for preserving DNA in the human and animal remains that have also been entombed there by local residents over the millennia.

I suppose it is fitting that a few days before Charles Darwin's 209th birthday in 2018 we learned from DNA extracted from one of the skeletal remains in a Cheddar cave that some, maybe most, native Englishmen ten thousand years ago were black. That is, they had black or very dark skin. It wasn't just England. Many native Europeans of that time were dark-skinned. If that discovery undermines something about your idea of race, good.

I say it is fitting because Darwin had a lifelong interest in human races and their origin.

To a naturalist like Darwin, race was a common way to describe obvious physical differences among geographically distinct populations of the same species. We do this all the time in animals. For instance, east of the Rocky Mountains, a bird species called the Northern Flicker is known to the ornithological world as the yellow-shafted race, yellow being the color of the underside of its wings and tail. West of the Rocky Mountains, there is a red-shafted race of the same species. The reason we call them separate races rather than different species is that where the two populations come together, they easily and often interbreed. Interbreeding, however, is confined to that narrow region. Genes for yellow- and red- underwings remain separated east and west of the Rockies.

Race as it applies to birds or bears or orchids is easy to describe and discuss. Race as it applies to humans is not. Race, often referring primarily to skin color, has been used to justify slavery, genocide, and social discrimination for centuries, which is why the discovery of black native Englishmen so nicely illustrates that for modern humans at least biological race is a fiction.

On Darwin's round-the-word voyage aboard the *Beagle* as a young man, he encountered a wider range of human diversity than most men of his time, spending some time among the native inhabitants of several parts of South America, Tahiti, and Australia. He spent most time with people from Tierra del Fuego, Fuegians as he called them, from the wind-swept, stormy, island archipelago at the southern tip of South America. Three Fuegians, a man, a boy, and a girl, had been kidnapped by the captain of the *Beagle*, Robert Fitzroy, eighteen months before Darwin's voyage. They were hauled off to England, dressed in English clothes, taught English manners and language, sent to English schools and church. On Darwin's voyage, they were being returned home in the hope that they might Christianize their own people and teach them civilized English habits.

Darwin was not particularly fixated on skin color, mentioning it almost in passing during his travels. He came from a family of ardent abolitionists at a time when slavery was still tolerated in much of the world. But he was very interested in social customs and habits of the native people he met. He particularly focused on habits that Victorian Englishmen valued as markers of a civilized society, such as gardening, good houses, cleanliness, modesty, and proper manners, none of which the Fuegians had. Their customs were about survival in the hostile environment in which they lived.

But people seemingly from time immemorial *have* been fixated on skin color as indicative of biological race, something that has been thoroughly undercut by recent genetic discoveries. Researchers have now analyzed the genomes of enough people around the world to identify gene variants that are most responsible for our rich palette of skin colors from pale white to ebony. These variants from across the color spectrum, we now know, originated in Africa a very long time ago, before modern humans had evolved. Neanderthals and even earlier human-like species likely had dark- and light-skinned individuals and every hue in between from the same African gene variants responsible for our skin colors today.

Black-skinned Britons seem to have been part of a migration wave of hunter-gatherers who left Africa around sixty thousand years ago, paused in the Middle East, and then swept across Europe some fifteen thousand years ago. Several thousand years after that, another wave of migrants (some might say "invaders"), this time of people who had developed farming, rolled in from what today is Turkey and Greece, bringing with them a different mixture of African skin color genes, which mixed and mingled with those of the earlier immigrants. Once again, about five thousand years ago, a third wave, this time of livestock herding people from the grasslands of western Russia, spread through Europe. Each migrant wave brought its own unique mix of genes, including a fresh mix of skin color genes derived from our distant African ancestors. Because of these repeated invasions, Europe for millennia like the United States today, is a complex medley of genes from many parts of the world.

Cheddar man is still with us in a sense. British people still contain about 10 percent of Cheddar man people's DNA. In fact, a genetic study of people currently living in the area around the Cheddar cave discovered a high school teacher, Adrian Targett, is a direct descendent of Cheddar man on his mother's side. Someone did point out that Mr. Targett looks nothing at all like his distant ancestor, especially his skin color. That is true, of course. But that seems to me the whole point.

Biological Clocks

THE 2017 Nobel Prize in Physiology or Medicine was awarded to three scientists who discovered why flies sleep best during the night. That's the way the award might be described by scientifically illiterate politicians (you know who you are) anyway, trying to outrage a scientifically illiterate base around the silly things that scientists waste their time and your money studying. In reality, the Prize was awarded for figuring out how biological clocks work. Flies have those clocks of course but so do you. What is a biological clock and why should you, and why did the Nobel Prize award committee, care?

Biological clocks keep flies or mice or people on an approximately twenty-four hour schedule without requiring any outside information such as whether it is day or night. Flies kept in a constantly dark incubator or people living deep in lightless caves still sleep, wake, and eat on an approximately twenty-four hour cycle.

The Nobel Prize was awarded for was figuring out how such clocks work, what genes made them tick, so to speak. It is much easier and quicker to discover the working of genes in flies than in mammals like us. The simplified version of how these clocks work is that clock genes in the brain, when turned on, produce a substance that when enough of it has accumulated turns the same genes off. That substance is gradually degraded, and when enough of it has disappeared, the genes turn back on again. That cycle of on-off gene activity occurs over approximately twenty-four hours in virtually all animals, even single-cell animals, and affects nearly every aspect of your biology.

Once these genes were discovered operating in this twenty-four hour cycle in fly brains, it became easier to look at other species such as ourselves to see if they had similar genes and if so, whether those genes behaved similarly. Yes, we do and yes, they do.

Now came some surprises. Clocks were discovered not only in fly brains but in many other parts of the fly too—wings, legs, and antennae, for instance. In people this is also true. Your main clock is located in a tiny brain region called the suprachiasmatic nucleus, but like flies you have local clocks almost everywhere. For instance, your liver, lungs, heart, muscles and immune system all have their own clocks. Even your individual cells operate on their own clock time. Cells tend to repair themselves at certain hours and are most prone to divide at certain times.

The medical implications of having all these clocks are profound. They imply, for instance, that there may be certain times of day (or night) at which medications will be most (or least) effective, so attention should be likely paid to when during the day you get your flu shot or your cancer chemotherapy. In my own field, the biology of aging, evidence is accumulating that the *timing* of when you eat may be as important for maintaining your health as what you eat.

It is the job of your brain's main clock to coordinate the activities of all the body's other clocks. Its own time is set by light. For most species, and for people over nearly all of our own history, the clock was set by the daily appearance of sunlight at dawn and its disappearance at dusk. However, in modern times we have invented endlessly creative ways to disrupt our clocks. We fly across multiple time zones, and so experience day and night at times for which our bodies are not prepared. We work under bright lights or stare at bright television or computer screens long after the sun has gone down. We even send people into space where, orbiting the earth, they can experience ninety minute day/night cycles for months at a time. Aging disrupts clocks too.

Clock disruption not surprisingly has health effects. Nighttime shift workers are well-known to be at higher risk than the rest of us for insomnia, obesity, diabetes, heart disease, ulcers, bowel and stomach problems, depression, dementia, and some types of cancer. However because we increasingly understand how our biological clocks work, medical practices are likely to change to make use of these biological rhythms. Researchers too are now working on clock-regulating medications to protect us against the dangers of clock disruption.

All this, because a few scientists noticed that flies like people sleep best at night and wondered why.

Eclipsing Superstition

I HAVE yet to meet anyone who doubts that a total solar eclipse will sweep across America from Texas to Maine on April 8, 2024, just as one swept across America from Oregon to South Carolina on August 21, 2017. In fact, hundreds of thousands, maybe millions, of people will no doubt travel by plane, train, and automobile specifically to watch the 2024 eclipse just as many, including me, did in 2017. Eclipse-deniers, so far as I can tell, do not exist.

I've been wondering why in this particular realm no one doubts the science.

Yet when the same scientists, who can predict this eclipse with such precision, and even predict exactly when and where the next ones will occur years or even centuries beforehand, tell us that the earth is 4.6 billion years old, millions of people feel confident that the scientists are wrong.

What this shows, I'm afraid, is how strong a grip superstition still has on the human mind even here in the twenty-first century. The occurrence of an eclipse does not conflict with anyone's superstitions. In fact, eclipses have been the *source* of a barrelful of superstitions. The real age of the earth, on the other hand, conflicts with many superstitions. And when superstition conflicts with science, for many—maybe most—people, it is the science that has to go.

I was pondering this pick-and-choose mentality when it comes to science acceptance on a recent airplane flight after I embarrassed myself by plopping down in the wrong seat. My actual seat was in row fourteen and having glanced up as I passed row twelve, I counted two more rows and sat down. Only after being asked to move, did I notice that the plane had no row thirteen which is why arithmetic failed me. On the same trip, I noticed that my hotel had a twelfth and fourteenth, but no thirteenth floor. Ah, superstitions.

The silliness of being afraid of a certain number should be obvious. Yet some sophisticated designer of airplanes and hotels either personally feared the number thirteen, or more likely, felt that enough people did that it should be avoided. In a number of Asian countries, I'm told, the number four is similarly avoided in numbering the floors of buildings.

I am not sure when the number thirteen came to be considered unlucky. Triskaidekaphobia, the official name for fear of the number thirteen, is said to have something to do with the fact that there were thirteen people present at Jesus' Last Supper although it has also been attributed to a thirteen person dinner in Norse mythology and perhaps also to something having to do with an ancient Babylonian law code. I do know that, thankfully, there was an eventual rebellion against this superstition when a group of prominent New Yorkers formed The Thirteen Club. These personal heroes of mine purposely held their first dinner with thirteen people on Friday the thirteenth. They dined on the thirteenth floor and had to walk under a ladder to enter the room. They also dined amid piles of spilled salt. That is an attitude toward superstition you have to respect.

It isn't surprising that we all have a few superstitions. I admit that I do. For instance, as a school boy baseball player, after each of my very rare home runs, I always carefully checked where I had flung my mitt before heading to bat, making sure that next time I stepped up to the plate, I placed the mitt in precisely the same place and position *just in case* it might have been the mitt placement rather than sheer luck that led to the home run. Strategic mitt placement couldn't salvage my baseball career though.

The human brain evolved during a time when it might have made sense to attribute meaning to random events. If someone was struck by lightning while standing under a certain tree then it might have made sense, and it certainly didn't hurt, to avoid standing under that tree in the future.

But that was then, this is now. Now we have a better grip on how and why things happen, cause and effect, thanks to science. Having a few superstitions is just part of our psychological heritage from those ancient days on the African savanna. That we still have superstitions is not surprising, but they shouldn't rule our lives. It's the twenty-first century, not the tenth.

In addition to conflicting with superstition, the other time when science is selectively denied is when it forces us to re-evaluate our own wonderfulness.

Science has shown us with all the clarity with which it can predict eclipses, that we shared a common ancestor with chimpanzees about six million years ago. Science is also quite clear that we are warming our planet by pouring more and more greenhouse gases into the atmosphere. However, these established scientific facts challenge the self-image or common habits of many people, so they convince themselves that the science must be wrong.

I personally don't find it demeaning that I'm a close evolutionary relative of a chimpanzee. A lot of people apparently do though.

But if you have spent any time closely watching chimpanzees, the resemblance is pretty clear. Their hands resemble ours, their facial expressions resemble ours, and like us they are devilishly clever. In some mental tasks, they even outperform us. Then, of course, there is the increasingly complete fossil record that shows the farther back in time you trace human ancestry, the more chimpanzee-like we become. When DNA sequencing came along it surprised no one in the scientific community when our genome turned out to be more similar to chimpanzees' genome than to any other species.

If we feel our human dignity challenged by our resemblance to chimpanzees, we feel even more aggrieved when told that our irresponsible collective behavior in burning fossil fuels is heating up our atmosphere and acidifying our oceans. This should not be news either. It is Chemistry 101 as pointed out as early as 1896 by the Nobel Prize-winner Swedish chemist, Svante Arrhenius. Now the evidence that Arrhenius was right is all around us. If you don't believe me, ask any penguin.

So everyone agrees that science can predict eclipses with phenomenal exactitude far into the future. Science led us to invent vehicles to whisk people hundreds of miles to watch those eclipses and developed glasses so that we wouldn't fry our eyes when doing so. Science has nearly doubled our lifespan in the past century, created technologies to make those lives increasingly pleasant, sent rockets to the distant reaches of the solar system, and returned photographs to earth from those rockets. But when it comes to understanding our own history or predicting the future of our own planet, you just can't trust science. Can you?

The Science of Ghosts

I FIND it rather breathtaking that in the healthiest countries in the world life expectancy has been increasing at the average rate of six hours per day for almost two centuries! A large part of the reason for that progress has to do with our better understanding of ghosts. I don't mean ghosts in the supernatural, from-beyond-the-grave sense. I mean ghosts in the sense of invisible beings with the power to do us great good or harm. Those ghosts can now be seen with the appropriate ghost detector, which is a good microscope.

Remember that for most of human history, sickness and death often struck haphazardly and without warning. Your spouse, child, or uncle would be fine until one day they were struck by a fever or terrible diarrhea, took to their beds, and died shortly thereafter. What else to blame but the spirit world? Besides if you had any enemies in the village, you could blame them for calling up such spirits, and with enough support from your neighbors could schedule a nice witch-roasting for weekend entertainment.

Before microscopes, we were at the mercy of our five senses. If our food or water looked and smelled all right, it must *be* all right. If a physician amputated a limb or treated an infection by drawing a few ounces of blood and the patient didn't die right away, that must be all right too. If the air smelled clean, it must be healthful. Open windows were considered a boon to health. It was well understood that foul odors were often associated with disease and the prevailing medical notion was that disease outbreaks were attributable to bad air.

Then French chemist Louis Pasteur came along and in the mid-nineteenth century demonstrated beyond all doubt that everything—air, earth, water, plants, animals, food, drink— was awash with organisms invisible to the naked eye and undetectable by the nose, and that these "micro" organisms were not merely bystanders to the visible world, they often ruled it. Micro-organisms caused our meat to rot, and our fruit and milk to spoil, and thankfully, for our wine to ferment, among other things.

Pasteur also theorized that micro-organisms that don't normally live inside us can cause diseases when they do manage to get inside our bodies. The idea that invisible germs cause disease is so well-established today that it is easy to forget what life was like prior to this discovery. People dug latrines next to their drinking water supplies and commonly left food exposed to flies and other vermin around for days without refrigeration before eating it. Physicians would treat one patient after another or perform a surgery, then an autopsy, then go back for another surgery, using the same bloody hands and bloody instruments. Washing hands and cleaning instruments between patients or procedures was not given a thought.

To read the diaries of famous people prior to the discovery that germs caused diseases is to read a litany of chronic illness—bouts of coughing, weakness, fever, or diarrhea that lasted for weeks or months, and often killed. George Washington, for instance, suffered from a series of such near-fatal infectious illnesses throughout his life. They confined him to bed for weeks at a time in the years before he became our first President. Such an infection, combined with the medical practice that was standard treatment at the time, did eventually kill him. Such infections also killed his great grandfather and great grandmother, his grandfather and grandmother, his father, his father's first wife, both his wife's parents, a half-sister, a half-brother. You get the idea.

As micro-organisms fill the air, some of them put there by coughing or sneezing sick people, the idea that bad air was the source of many diseases wasn't completely crazy. Airborne transmission of disease was responsible for some of our major scourges, such as tuberculosis, smallpox, anthrax, flu, measles, chickenpox, and today's COVID-19, for instance. But of course it wasn't the air, it was the germs in the air that were at fault.

Food- and waterborne diseases, such as E. coli-contaminated spinach or Salmonella-contaminated ice cream, that sicken, or even kill, a few dozen people make news headlines today. They make headlines because they are rare events. Two centuries ago, they would have never been noticed against the massive background of such diseases that killed thousands of people on a daily basis.

Pasteur taught us not only that ghosts cause disease, but that many of them could be killed by appropriate hygiene. The first ghostbuster was soap and water. Heat (pasteurization) or chemicals could also kill unseen germs. By the early twentieth century public water supplies were filtered and chemically-treated, making them much safer. Freezing and refrigeration, thanks to the widespread availability of electricity, made stored food safer too. By World War II we had developed drugs called antibiotics that killed bacteria. Surviving common infections due to food, water, air, or wounds became almost assured. We had largely conquered our ghosts.

For that, we might give a silent thanks to Louis Pasteur, the biggest ghostbuster of them all, and the man who probably has saved more lives than anyone in history.

49269230R00146